"In this wonderful book, Luke gives us a wonderful blend of solid research, personal narratives, and practical guidance for anyone who is on the path to develop a new faith community that is a Fresh Expression. I am happy to recommend this treasure to church planters and mentees, and will be using it as required reading for courses I teach about developing new faith communities."

— Elaine A. Heath, PhD, President, Neighborhood Seminary

"With the dawn of a post-COVID new wineskin reality, *Becoming Church* is a needed contribution and practical guide for those determined not to return to the church of old."

— Hugh Halter, Author of *The Tangible Kingdom*, *Flesh*, and *AND: The Gathered and Scattered Church*

"Church among other things, has become so complex. Complex is easy . . . and paralyzing. Simple is hard! What Luke Edwards brings is a refreshing and insightful guide to new and necessary forms of church. This book shows the hard work that has been done to make the complicated simple and the principles practical. I believe this is a must read for all church leaders!"

— Brian Zehr, Former Pastor at Community Christian Church (Chicagoland) and Leadership Architect of International Impact

"Luke Edwards embodies the humble, thoughtful leadership so many of us crave today. He recenters the church in its most essential values of cultivating real community and offering a healing space for members. Readers will find Luke's perspective refreshing and his writing equally graceful and accessible."

— Bailey Richardson, Partner at People & Company and Co-Author of *Get Together: How to Build a Community with Your People*

"A good trail guide provides basic information about the route, and practical, experienced-based advice from someone who has made the journey. In *Becoming Church*, Luke Edwards delivers these well, and adds personal, pastoral, and theological reflections. We'll be making sure our practitioners have this resource in their trail gear."

— David Guthrie, President, Provincial Elders' Conference, Moravian Church in America, Southern Province

"*Becoming Church* is a great book that weaves together a rich tapestry of real-life examples, practical insights and principles of how to do fresh expressions of church. It is well written and presented in a way that is both humorous and down to earth, while still being easy to read. Luke's wide experience of fresh expressions begins through his own journey pioneering King Street Church, Boone—a new church that met in a pub and became family for many unchurched people. Luke's experience then widened further through his involvement in many other fresh expressions in North Carolina. Luke's resulting book, *Becoming Church*, is a must-read not only for those beginning to explore fresh expressions of church but also for those already involved, who've been on the pioneering journey for a while."

— Andy Milne, Missional Youth Church Network Strategic Lead, Office of the Archbishop of York

"*Becoming Church* maps out that trail connecting romantic dreams with practical reality, written by an experienced guide who has traversed that expanse multiple times. It is an enjoyable, accessible read for the masses and a good reference for those who want to go further."

— Randy Weener, Director of Church Multiplication, Reformed Church in America

"This resource is at once intensely practical while simultaneously, refreshingly non-prescriptive. With heart, a healthy dose of humility, and great wisdom that comes from experience, Luke lays out a course for what it really takes to foster new faith communities. If you've wanted to follow God into your community, but have been unsure what to do, this is the book that will catapult you from talking about it to actually doing something about it."

— Shannon Kiser, Director of Training, Fresh Expressions US, Pastor, Riverside Presbyterian Church, Sterling, VA

"The beauty of *Becoming Church* is how approachable and practical it is. Here is a model for starting new Christian communities independent of big egos and budgets. A model for ordinary people like you and me. Luke is clear and direct in communicating his vision for starting expressions of church that reach those who otherwise would not find their way to established congregations. Read this, and then get started."

— Jason Evans, Missioner for Missional Communities, Episcopal Diocese of Texas

"Luke Edwards offers us a much-needed metaphor for the church today: a community of imperfect people following

Jesus on a hiking adventure! This vision of what the church can and should be calls us to embrace a posture of vulnerability, courage, and hope in a time of massive change. Luke is a practitioner who has been involved with the Fresh Expressions movement in the US from the beginning. This trail guide is the cumulative wisdom of someone who has walked the journey with others and is now showing us paths in the wild of a new frontier. Grab your team and get your hiking boots!"

— Michael Adam Beck, Author, Pastor, Professor, and Cultivator of Movements; Director of the Fresh Expressions House of Studies at United Theological Seminary; Director of Remissioning Fresh Expressions US; and Cultivator of Fresh Expressions Florida UMC

"Are you experiencing a nudge to imagine and then embody a new way to be church in our postmodern world? This short yet detailed book by Luke Edwards is a vital guide to help you move from a vision to reality. Edwards's book is grounded in an understanding that new expressions of church return to the image of the crowd that followed Jesus during his earthly ministry. A church that is a "porous, loosely organized group of broken people following Christ wherever he goes, a community on a journey." Theologically sound yet profoundly practical, this is a book I highly recommend. You will return to it often as you move into the beautiful yet messy process of *Becoming Church*."

— Rev. Roberta J. Egli, Executive Director, Messy Church USA

"In the near future, if I plan to visit and enjoy the best trails and sceneries of the Appalachian Trail, I will definitely ask

Luke to come with me. He is married to an Appalachian Trail family! However, if one desires to discover the new trails of how to start fresh expressions in their backyard, or anywhere in the USA, you will find that *Becoming Church* is the book to get your feet going on the right path. In his book, Luke guides you through all phases of the innovative progression of Fresh Expressions from start to completion. And he does so with such exquisite, adventurous spirit and with an excellent array of academic guides whom you can converse with on your journey!"

— Rev. Dr. Eliseo A. Mejia, Senior Pastor of Paris First UMC, National Director of Expresiones Divinas (FX-US), Church-Planting Leader, and Missiologist

"Becoming Church is a real, timely look at what it looks like to be the church outside of church, walking alongside people from all walks of life. So much in here is applicable to all leaders and followers of Christ, not just those who are interested in fresh expressions. I was laughing, crying, and covered in chill bumps thinking about how bright the future of the church is as we embrace more fresh expressions of faith."

— Rachel "Dragonfly" Ahrens, 2020 Appalachian Trail Chaplain

A **FRESH EXPRESSIONS** BOOK

BECOMING CHURCH

A Trail Guide for Starting Fresh Expressions

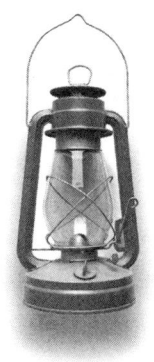

Richmond, Virginia

Becoming Church: A Trail Guide for Starting Fresh Expressions
Copyright © 2021 by Luke S. Edwards

Requests for information should be sent via e-mail to info@freshexpressionsus.com. Visit freshexpressionsus.org for contact information.

All Scripture quotations, unless otherwise indicated, are taken from the Holy Bible, New International Version®, NIV®. Copyright ©1973, 1978, 1984, 2011 by Biblica, Inc.® Used by permission of Zondervan. All rights reserved worldwide. www.zondervan.com. The "NIV" and "New International Version" are trademarks registered in the United States Patent and Trademark Office by Biblica, Inc.®

Scripture quotations marked MSG are taken from THE MESSAGE. Copyright © 1993, 2002, 2018 by Eugene H. Peterson. Used by permission of NavPress. All rights reserved. Represented by Tyndale House Publishers, a Division of Tyndale House Ministries.

Any internet addresses (websites, blogs, etc.) in this book are offered as a resource. They are not intended in any way to be or imply an endorsement by Fresh Expressions US; nor does Fresh Expressions US vouch for the content of these sites and contact numbers for the life of this book.

All rights reserved. No part of this book, including icons and images, may be reproduced in any manner without prior written permission from the copyright holder, except where noted in the text and in the case of brief quotations embodied in critical articles and reviews.

The spelling of words in the Foreword by Bishop Graham Cray, with his consent, and in some quotations throughout the book has been modified for American readers.

ISBN 978-1-7345081-0-9 (Paperback)
ISBN - 978-1-7345081-4-7 (Kindle)
ISBN - 978-1-7345081-4-7 (ePub)

Cover design: Ryan Tate

Interior design, illustrations, and typesetting: Harrington Interactive Media (harringtoninteractive.com)

Printed in the United States of America

For Mary Frances,
may you find community with God and with God's people
in whatever form of church it may be.

CONTENTS

Foreword by Bishop Graham Cray 13
Acknowledgements 17

1. Preparing for the Journey 19
2. Listening 37
3. Loving People 59
4. Building Community 77
5. Exploring Discipleship 101
6. Church Taking Shape 127
7. Doing It Again 151
8. Flip-Flops and Final Thoughts 173

About the Author 189

LISTENING → LOVING PEOPLE → BUILDING COMMUNITY → EXPLORING DISCIPLESHIP → CHURCH TAKING SHAPE → DOING IT AGAIN

UNDERPINNED BY PRAYER AND CONTINUING CONNECTION TO THE WIDER CHURCH

FOREWORD

This book is a joy to read and to recommend. It is full of insight born from experience. I recognize so much of what Luke has written, and yet it's also new to me, because the context for which Luke has written is different from the context in which the fresh expressions ministry was born. The work in the US has grown into something distinctive. I have never walked the Appalachian Trail (though I have canoed a little part of the Buffalo, when the water level was really low!). But the metaphor came alive as I read Luke's book, and it gave me fresh light for the continuing missional pilgrimage in the UK.

During my time as the Fresh Expressions team leader, American friends, who had recognized the relevance of the fresh expressions work for their contexts, asked to link up with us and to share our materials. Our answer was an enthusiastic *Yes, But* (typical Brits!). *Yes,* we'd be delighted to have you partner with us. *Yes,* of course you can use our materials. *But* there is one condition: you *must* change them. As you work this out for your context you must replace our stories with your stories, our materials with the ones you create, and our contextual insights for yours, as you follow the Holy Spirit in this creative ecclesial adventure. That is what has happened, and it has been a joy to watch. Fresh Expressions US is a mature, indigenous, missional movement, from which I continue to learn. This book is part of the fruit of it.

In the UK this all began with a committee writing a report on church planting for the governing body of a traditional denomination—the Church of England. I chaired the group. The report was called "Mission-Shaped Church," and it coined the term "fresh expressions of church." The team our Archbishop created to carry the work forward then identified, from frontline experience, the beginnings of the praxis that Luke describes in this book and has adapted for its new context in the US.

Luke's book is full of practical wisdom, based on his and other practitioners' experience. It follows a sequence I recognize, and which has proved to be transcultural. In what context do you not need to listen to the Spirit, make friends, form communities, make disciples, and so on?

The practices he describes are important, but I invite you to do more than learn the practices. More important still, take on board the underlying vision and values, as he has done.

Early in our committee's time we were powerfully impacted by this Scripture.

> Now there were some Greeks among those who went up to worship at the festival. They came to Philip, who was from Bethsaida in Galilee, with a request. "Sir," they said, "we would like to see Jesus." Philip went to tell Andrew; Andrew and Philip in turn told Jesus. Jesus replied, "The hour has come for the Son of Man to be glorified. Very truly I tell you, unless a kernel of wheat falls to the ground and dies, it remains only a single seed. But if it dies, it produces many seeds." (John 12:20–24)

The passage speaks of the necessity of the cross for our salvation. One had to die for all. But an analogy struck us forcefully. If today's "Greeks"—people outside of both God's covenant and the specific culture of God's people—were not only to see Jesus but also to follow him, then there needed to be another dying. We called it "dying to live." The planter or planting team has to be willing to "die" to their previous church culture, so the fresh expression it establishes will be culturally appropriate to its context. We wrote, "Dying to live is inherent in the planting process." The object of the journey is not church as we would like it, nor church as we think it ought to be. In fact, it is not about church for us at all. It's about church for them, for their context, so they can see it transformed by Jesus.

That is the challenge of fresh expressions of church. Luke has set out the vision, the practices, and the values. I invite you to set out on the trail with him as your trustworthy guide.

Bishop Graham Cray, November 2020

ACKNOWLEDGEMENTS

There are so many people to thank for helping make this book happen. I want to thank Dave Wintsch, who was the first person to show me that a Christian community marked by acceptance and delight is possible. I am grateful to Joe Bova, who first helped me discern a call to serve the church. I thank all my friends from King Street Church—the family we built together has changed me forever (mostly for the better) and has given me a vision of all that Christian community can be. I thank Vern Collins and the people of Boone UMC who invested in me and gave me a chance to try something new. I am grateful to Dan Pezet, John Boggs, Lory Beth Huffman, Bishop Paul Leeland, and many others in the Western North Carolina Conference who supported King Street Church from its beginning and trusted me to cultivate our fresh expressions movement here in western North Carolina. I thank all the leaders of fresh expressions in western North Carolina whose work inspires me daily. I thank Chris Backert, Shannon Kiser, Chris Morton, Michael Beck, and all of my friends at Fresh Expressions US for their support and insights that made this book possible. I also thank Bishop Graham Cray, Michael Moynagh, Andy Milnes, and many others from Fresh Expressions UK who have helped lay the groundwork for the global fresh expressions movement. I thank Dustin Mailman and Chuck and Elissa Huffstetler for their friendship and their help in making this book better. I am eternally grateful to Jason Byassee for his friendship, mentorship, and gracious guidance as an editor throughout the process of writing this book. I thank Joe Breen, who—with the help of the Holy Spirit and the wisdom of Ignatius—kept my soul intact through this difficult season. Lastly, I am grateful to my family, especially my wife, Ginna, who patiently supported my writing process as we navigated work, writing, and parenthood in the midst of a global pandemic. I can't imagine walking this trail without you beside me.

Chapter One

PREPARING FOR THE JOURNEY

"The Bible is fundamentally a story of a people's journey with God."
— Stanley Hauerwas and Will Willimon

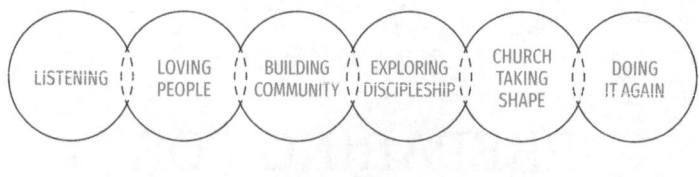

UNDERPINNED BY PRAYER AND CONTINUING CONNECTION TO THE WIDER CHURCH

I married into an Appalachian Trail family. The iconic trail meanders 2,190 miles from Georgia to Maine. When you hike the trail, you are given a nickname by fellow hikers, called a *trail name*. My brother-in-law is a thru-hiker, someone who hikes the entirety of the trail in one journey over the course of five to seven months. His trail name is "Flash" because he hiked in a kilt and wasn't used to keeping his legs together as he sat around camp. My mother-in-law is a section hiker, someone who hikes a section at a time and completes the trail over the course of several years. Her nickname is "Sash," a nod to over a decade of leading a Girl Scout troop. My father-in-law, who has quietly supported (and partially funded) both of their journeys, has his own honorary trail name, "Cash."

There's something intrinsically spiritual about a journey like hiking the Appalachian Trail. For millennia, Christians have gone for long walks in search of spiritual transformation. Since the fourth century, pilgrims have traveled routes like the Via Francigena from Canterbury to Rome, the Camino de Santiago across northern Spain, and various routes ending at Jerusalem.[1] Pilgrimage is the original thru-hike. There's an

---

1. The earliest recorded Christian pilgrimage to Jerusalem is the *Itinerarium Burdigalense*, 333 CE. See Jaś Elsner, "The Itinerarium Burdigalense: Politics and Salvation in the Geography of Constantine's Empire," *Journal of Roman Studies* 90 (2000): 181–95.

expectation that on the other end of a 2,000-mile walk you will be a different person, that along the way you will discover something of significance about the world and about yourself. Pope Benedict puts it this way: "To go on pilgrimage really means to step out of ourselves in order to encounter God where he has revealed himself, where his grace has shone with particular splendor."[2]

There's a deep call within us to journey. It is motion that makes us human. Throughout the Bible, the people of God are constantly on the move together, following the God revealed in a pillar of cloud and a pillar of fire, following Jesus through the Judean countryside, following the prompting of the Holy Spirit to the far reaches of the known world. We are indeed a "Pilgrim Church."[3]

The Church of Scotland says the church's core calling is "to be people with Jesus at the center, traveling where Jesus takes us."[4] The first time I heard this was in a training with Bishop Graham Cray, who led the fresh expressions movement in England from 2008 to 2014. Later in the training, he added:

> I'm increasingly looking to the gospel image of Christ on the move through the countryside with his disciples as the image of church. Not only was it the 12 disciples, it was the women, it was the 70, and more. Surely some

---

2. Pope Benedict XVI, "Address of the Holy Father Benedict XVI," *The Vatican*, November 6, 2010, w2.vatican.va/content/benedict-xvi/en/speeches/2010/november/documents/hf_ben-xvi_spe_20101106_cattedrale-compostela.html.
3. Pope Paul VI, "Lumen Gentium," *The Vatican*, November 21, 1964, vatican.va/archive/hist_councils/ii_vatican_council/documents/vat-ii_const_19641121_lumen-gentium_en.html.
4. The General Assembly of the Church of Scotland, "A Church Without Walls," *Church of Scotland*, 2001, 8, churchofscotland.org.uk/__data/assets/pdf_file/0006/11787/CWW_REPORT_for_website_2Nov2012.pdf.

> of them were questioning, wondering if Christ's claims were true.[5]

In the image of the crowd following Jesus through the Judean countryside, we find a picture of what the church could be: a porous, loosely organized group of broken people following Christ wherever he goes—a community on a journey. We're hungry. He feeds us. We're sick. He heals our diseases. He dies for us, rises, and makes us a new humanity. The invitation to join such a church resonates with our postmodern world—an invitation to walk with others as we follow Jesus together. There's a recognition within such an invitation that we have not yet arrived, we don't hold all the answers, but we're on a journey to the kingdom. Won't you join us?

From Charity to Community

In the fall of 2009, as an idealistic college student learning about poverty and hunger, I began an impassioned endeavor to solve all of my neighbors' problems. I helped my church start a firewood ministry, a community garden, and a home repair ministry serving impoverished neighbors throughout our county in the Appalachian Mountains of North Carolina. Four years later, I was a burned-out missions pastor with a waning savior complex who realized that despite my best efforts, my neighbors' situations were relatively unchanged. Eventually, I realized the problem: We had built efficient relief programs, but we had never built community with our neighbors. We viewed our neighbors as recipients instead of friends. And without creating community, we had failed to see the larger systemic problems holding our neighbors back. The relationships we'd formed were marred by unequal power,

---

5. Bishop Graham Cray, *Fresh Expressions US National Gathering* (April 2016).

codependency, and manipulation. It was in the midst of this realization that I was invited by my senior pastor and supervisor to start a new worshiping community in the downtown area of Boone. Later that year, King Street Church was born.

At King Street Church we gathered a group of people who were interested in talking about faith and life but were not interested in going to church. We formed a community made up of those who were Christian and those who were not sure what they believed. Every week we gathered at the local pub, opened a Bible, and talked about how this ancient text connected with our everyday lives.

Over the next six years we became a network of fresh expressions, meeting in pubs, coffee shops, the county jail, and the area homeless shelter. The local paper described us as "a small, nomadic worshiping community." By our third year, our church was largely composed of folks with criminal records looking to navigate life after incarceration. For the first time in my ministry, I witnessed neighbors experiencing liberation. Just as I had suspected years before, this liberation occurred in the context of community. Members would often call King Street Church their family (even if it was often a dysfunctional one). When we gathered, the voices of our members who were marginalized were heard and amplified, and we were able to come together to address oppressive systems holding our friends back. When I was a missions pastor, I was trying to fix social problems with solutions I had come up with. When I was in community with those recently released from incarceration, we looked for solutions together. Ever since, I've worked to help churches shift their energy from populating their preconceived programs to building communities with their neighbors where they grow friendships, encounter Christ, and experience liberation.

I remember our first Holy Week as a newly formed fresh expression. Our journey had begun the previous summer when my friend and I gathered a dozen of our friends, mostly in their twenties. Every week we would meet at someone's apartment to devour a casserole and talk about a passage from Scripture. It was the evening of Good Friday and the sun had set. Ten of us met at the trailhead of a three-mile hiking loop on the edge of town. My brilliant idea was to lead a "Stations of the Cross Hike." I'd been to seminary—I knew how to manipulate people into a religious experience. We would hike up the steep, wooded trail for a few minutes, read a passage from the passion story, and hike a little more and read another passage. I asked everyone to hike silently to maintain a mood of solemnity. It was sure to be a powerful experience.

At the second stop, the unmistakable *kerrrr-pish* of a beer bottle opening sounded from the outskirts of our circled group. The group erupted into laughter as I groaned, "Really, guys?!" I'm not sure why it took me so long to realize this wasn't going to be like any church or ministry I had ever led and all of those ministry tricks I had learned were no longer of use to me. Everyone fought back giggles as we navigated the trail together in the darkness. This was our church—a group of broken, vulnerable (and thirsty) people journeying together, trying to find our way through the dark, walking with Christ, laughing along the way.

Fresh Expressions: The Prequels

This book is about how to start a fresh expression of church. It really should be the second book you read about fresh expressions. There are other books that spend a lot more pages describing what a fresh expression is and why we need them so desperately as a supplement to how the church has long done ministry.[6] If you need a refresher, or if you're just too cheap to buy another book, here's a quick overview:

Why do we need fresh expressions? Every year, between 660,000 and 700,000 Americans leave formal religion.[7] There is a mass exodus from the church in the United States, but interestingly enough, not away from spirituality. The number of Americans claiming to have mystical encounters with God has actually increased from 22 percent in 1962 to 48 percent in 2009.[8] The United States doesn't have a faith problem; it has a church problem.

What would happen if we were willing to start churches in a way that connected with this growing number of people? That's a question the Church of England asked almost twenty years ago.

So what is a fresh expression? The Fresh Expressions movement started in the Church of England in 2004 with a simple question: What do we need to have church? What is essential? The denomination, under the leadership of Rowan Williams, Archbishop of Canterbury at the time, studied a wave of innovative churches forming in response to increasing secularization in Britain. Churches were popping up in pubs, parks, and other community spaces among people who had never been to church before. As more information about these new forms of church emerged, they realized they were witnessing a movement of the Holy Spirit in their midst. The Church of England quickly surrounded the movement with resources and support. Tracing back to the sixth century, the Church of England is about as traditional a denomination as

---

6. I highly recommend Michael Adam Beck, *Deep Roots, Wild Branches: Revitalizing the Church in the Blended Ecology* (Franklin, TN: Seedbed, 2019).
7. Phil Zuckerman, *Living the Secular Life* (New York: Penguin, 2014), 60.
8. Diana Butler Bass, *Christianity After Religion: The End of Church and the Birth of a New Spiritual Awakening* (New York: HarperCollins, 2013), 3–4.

there is, yet they developed a language and understanding of church that helped these fresh expressions fit within the existing structure of traditional forms of church. Fresh expressions came to be officially defined as the following:

> A form of church for our changing culture, established primarily for the benefit of people who are not yet members of any church. It will come into being through principles of listening, service, incarnational mission and making disciples. It will have the potential to become a mature expression of church shaped by the gospel and the enduring marks of the church and for its cultural context.[9]

As the movement developed, five defining features of fresh expressions emerged that differentiate fresh expressions from other innovative ministries:

- *Missional*: A fresh expression exists primarily for people who do not attend church.
- *Contextual*: A fresh expression connects with people in ways that are specific to their culture and location.
- *Incarnational*: A fresh expression goes to where people are in the community.
- *Formational*: A fresh expression aims to make new disciples and help disciples grow in Christian maturity.
- *Ecclesial*: A fresh expression intends to become church with the people it connects with.

Fresh Expressions is now an international movement with thousands of faith communities introducing people to Christ

---

9. "Quick Look A02 - Mission Context," Fresh Expressions UK, 2017, freshexpressions.org.uk/resources-3/quick-look-guides/quick-look-a02-mission-context/.

in post-Christian settings around the world. In the United States nearly all fresh expressions are anchored to an existing church, which provides leadership, support, and accountability. The anchor church in turn receives the gift of becoming able to connect with people who would never come to church on Sunday morning. The new fresh expression and the older anchor church inform, renew, and bless one another. Rowan Williams borrowed a term from economics to call this reciprocal blessing a "mixed economy of church." Those of us who are hesitant to use economic terms have begun calling this a "blended ecology of church."[10]

Guideposts for the Journey

In the summer of 2007, my friends and I graduated from high school and piled into my 1967 Volkswagen Bus for a road trip through Maine that led us to Mt. Katahdin, the northern terminus of the Appalachian Trail. The five-mile hike from the campground is straight up a 5,000-foot mountain, and about halfway up you begin to climb over hundreds of boulders of varying size. Thoreau described this stretch as "a vast aggregation of loose rocks, as if some time it had rained rocks."[11] There is no well-worn path to follow. All you have is the occasional trail marker that Appalachian Trail hikers have relied on for two thousand miles—a white standing rectangle that a volunteer slabbed on rocks and trees with the quick swipe of a paintbrush.

Sometimes these white blazes can be pretty far apart. As we hiked in between markers, I would start to feel a little anxiety. *Did we get turned off of the trail?* I would wonder, *Will we need to survive on wild berries until the park rangers find us?*

---

10. See Beck's *Deep Roots, Wild Branches* for more.
11. Henry David Thoreau, *The Maine Woods* (Overland Park, KS: Digireads.com Publishing, 2019), 30.

After a few minutes the glorious sight of white paint would assure us that we were still heading in the right direction.

Trail markers are nothing new to the church. Monastic communities have lived for millennia with a *rule*, the community's agreed upon way of life (e.g., *The Rule of St. Benedict*). The Latin word we translate as "rule" is *regula*, which means guidepost. Guideposts are the collected wisdom of previous travelers that offer direction for our own journeys. They keep us from wandering off on other paths we might encounter along the way. For monks and nuns these guideposts pointed to a way of forming and growing a community that would be a foretaste of the kingdom of God.

As fresh expressions popped up throughout the UK, the leaders of the movement identified a path that most had traveled. This path became the six steps of "The Fresh Expressions Journey." These guideposts have shown the way for thousands of leaders of new forms of church, myself included, and I'm confident they will guide you too.

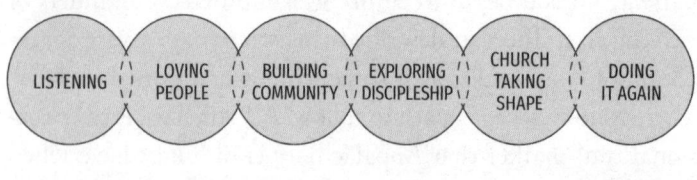

UNDERPINNED BY PRAYER AND CONTINUING CONNECTION TO THE WIDER CHURCH

Starting a fresh expression is a hard path to navigate. Without this resource I would have missed signs that our community was ready to take the next step in becoming church. Throughout this book, I will dedicate a chapter to each of these guideposts. I'll talk about their foundations in the life and ministry of Christ, and I'll talk about what they looked like in King Street Church and in other fresh expressions I

Chapter One | Preparing for the Journey

have worked with in western North Carolina and beyond. Each chapter ends with further readings (one Christian reading and one from an outside perspective) and a collect (a liturgical prayer like you might find in *The Book of Common Prayer*) to carry with you on each leg of the journey.[12]

For now, I'll give you a quick glimpse of each step:

Listening. The fresh expressions journey begins with attentive listening to a specific community, to our own interests and social connections, and to God. By listening to our community first, leaders discover the path to starting a church that will resonate with our neighbors.

Loving People. As the process of listening progresses, leaders look for opportunities to love others, deepen existing friendships, and form new friendships with people outside of the church. These are the folks we can invite into our newly forming community. Love is so central to the entire journey that the process is often referred to as a "loving-first journey."

Building Community. As relationships form between leaders of fresh expressions and their neighbors, a social gathering begins to take shape. These gatherings often begin around shared interests and meet in homes or community spaces.

Exploring Discipleship. This is the hardest transition to make. The leaders patiently look for opportunities to introduce discipleship to the group. Often, the best way for this to happen is to leave the social gathering untouched, inviting folks who have become a part of the group to come to an additional gathering with a simple element of discipleship. Some will come and some will not (and that's what keeps it from being manipulative, as we will see in Chapter 5).

---

12. Accompanying prayers are written by Terry Stokes, a recent graduate of Princeton Theological Seminary who writes modern collects that weave in contemporary issues and pop culture on his Instagram account @prayersfromterry.

Church Taking Shape. As disciples are formed, elements of church are added to the group. Elements like the sacraments, the study of Scripture, and worship are slowly incorporated into the budding fresh expression. As more marks of the church are included, the fresh expression of church moves closer to becoming a mature expression of church. Of course, different traditions will define in their own way what constitutes the complete picture of a church.

Doing It Again. After experiencing the process, every member of the fresh expression has the ability to start another one. Individual fresh expressions become networks of fresh expressions, and a movement is born.

Underpinned by Prayer and Continuing Connection to the Wider Church. Starting a fresh expression is a work of the Holy Spirit, and therefore the whole journey is marked by prayerful reflection and discernment. We should be praying as individuals, teams, and churches at every step of the fresh expressions journey. Additionally, most fresh expressions in the US are anchored to existing congregations that can provide leadership, support, and accountability.

While the fresh expressions journey looks neat and linear on paper, it's messier in practice. The stages are not always distinct. Listening carries through the whole journey, new relationships are often formed during listening, and you will see later that discipleship begins long before we explicitly talk about Christ. We are all starting in different places. Some readers will have many connections in their community and can gather folks quickly. Others will need to spend more time building new relationships. Every journey looks different. The fresh expressions journey stages are guideposts to help you move forward in the process of becoming church. They keep you heading in the right direction. Your trail companion, the Holy Spirit, is your true guide.

Many Appalachian Trail hikers carry torn out pages of the *AWOL Guidebook*, which lists water sources, campsites, and road crossings along the journey.[13] My hope is that after reading this book, you'll be able to recognize the markers around you as you journey forward into the great wilderness of post-Christendom. Maybe you will tear out a few of your favorite pages to carry with you as you go.

The Call of the Trail

My mother-in-law read about the Appalachian Trail when she was a young woman, and it captured her imagination, but she never thought she could actually hike it. Thirty years later, as her son set out for his thru-hike, she started thinking about it more and more—something she describes as "the call of the trail." She started doing the math and figured out that she could hike ten miles a day for three weeks for ten summers and complete the trail. When she mentioned the idea to her husband, he said, "Well, you're not getting any younger." She now has just 360 miles in New Hampshire and Maine left. The call of the trail pulled her out of her comfort zone and into a great wilderness.

Most good adventures begin with a little discontentment. "The call of the trail" stirs within us, calling us out of the status quo and into the wild and unpredictable. Perhaps you are discontented with the fact that your church hasn't welcomed in new members in a long time. Perhaps your gifts have never felt useful in the church, but this approach sounds different. We started King Street Church because we had friends who would never enter a traditional form of church. They needed

---

13. David Miller, *The A.T. Guide: A Handbook for Hiking the Appalachian Trail* (Wilmington, NC: AntiGravityGear, 2020). It's called the AWOL Guidebook in reference to the author's trail name.

something different. If you are feeling discontented, it could be the call to start something new. God often calls people to lead in ministry this way, via holy discontentment. What's important is that your discontentment is driven and guided by love and hope for something better, not stained by frustration and spite.

Starting a fresh expression is about building a community that is growing in God's love. It's not about getting what you want. As in other areas of life, some people seeking to start new religious communities are doing so because they want to be in control. Perhaps they didn't like the direction their last church was heading, or perhaps they disagreed with what was being taught. If your group's identity is based on being against something or someone else, then you might be starting a fresh expression for control. You will end up exerting that control over others to make the fresh expression what you want it to be. Let me tell you now, you are not in control when you start a fresh expression. Christ is, and it's going to be one heck of a ride. When you commit to starting a fresh expression, you are inviting Christ to create the kind of community Christ desires.

The reason I hear most often for starting a fresh expression is this: "I want to keep our church from dying." The church already has a Savior! If the end goal of a fresh expression is a program that will benefit your church, then you will see your neighbors as a means to an end. Dave Male puts it this way: "People are not targets to get into church, but creatures beloved by the Creator."[14] People are never to be used, only ever to be enjoyed as friends. Love of God and love of neighbor must be our motivation for starting fresh

---

14. David Male, *How to Pioneer: Even If You Haven't a Clue* (London: Church House Publishing, 2016), 41.

expressions. If you reflect on why you don't want your church to die, I would guess it's because it has meant something to you. Perhaps it has been a place of love and acceptance and a place to feel God's presence. Wanting others to experience that is an act of loving your neighbor, and it's a good reason to start a fresh expression. Go with that instead!

This book assumes that Christianity is Good News for the world and that we want more of it. I assume this because I have found an abundant life following Jesus alongside his motley friends. This book also assumes that the church, while entirely imperfect, is the primary vessel through which the kingdom of God is being revealed. If you are uninterested in growing Christians, or would rather critique Christianity or start something else, this book probably won't suit you. If your goal is to see the Good News of Christ come alive in our world today, let's walk together!

Cooking Class for Widowers

A few years back a denominational leader in Australia told me the story of one of his favorite fresh expressions. Two elderly women attended a fresh expressions training and decided to give it a try. As they reflected on their own gifts and began to think of those in their town who were in need of community, an idea came to them. Some of their friends who had passed away left husbands behind, and many of these widowers didn't know how to cook. They ate at restaurants or ate microwave meals every night, and many of them had become socially isolated. When they thought about these men, the women said to themselves, "We know how to cook; we could teach them." They reserved an industrial kitchen, put an ad in the local paper, and a few weeks later a dozen widowers showed up for their first cooking class. As they learned to cook, the group prepared a meal, and to close out their time, they ate together. As the class progressed over the coming weeks, they began to take prayer requests and pray together. The fresh expressions journey isn't just a pathway for hipsters allergic to religious institutions (though there are some of us). It's for all of us who long to draw our neighbors into the loving embrace of Christian community.

It's Your Journey

You're ready to start a fresh expression. It's why you're holding this book. The path forward from here will not be without its challenges, but you go with Christ and you go with thousands of others who have relied on the trail map called the fresh expressions journey. Every context is different and therefore there is no GPS for this journey, but there are trail markers if you know where to look. In starting King Street Church, and helping over 250 fresh expressions begin their journeys in western North Carolina, I have come to recognize the guideposts along this lightly worn path, and I'll do my best to point them out to you. It's your journey, but you don't have to make it alone. So lace up your hiking shoes and brace yourself for the unexpected. *Kerrrr-pish*.

Further Reading:

Michael Adam Beck, *Deep Roots, Wild Branches: Revitalizing the Church in the Blended Ecology* (Franklin, TN: Seedbed, 2019).

Beck offers a compelling argument for fresh expressions and describes how the blended ecology works. This is a near perfect introduction to fresh expressions and pairs well with the book you are currently holding in your hands.

Phil Zuckerman, *Living the Secular Life: New Answers to Old Questions* (New York: Penguin, 2014).

If you only read books about church decline that are written by Christians, you're missing some key perspectives. Zuckerman gives a glimpse into his secular and moral life and tells about his growing number of companions.

Accompanying Prayer
A Collect for the Journey

O Christ the Incarnate Word, you listened to us, came to us, befriended us, brought the kingdom of God to us, and then built the church on that foundation. Show us how to do the same with our neighbors, driven by a love that yearns not to control but to give itself up to the uncertainties of the journey. Lead us by guideposts made by those you have shepherded before us, but lead us ultimately to the place you have prepared for this particular community, by the Holy Spirit our Guide, who reigns with you and our Father, one God, renewing all things. *Amen.*

— Terry Stokes

Chapter Two

LISTENING

"Whether you turn to the right or to the left, your ears will hear a voice behind you, saying, 'This is the way; walk in it.'"
— Isaiah 30:21

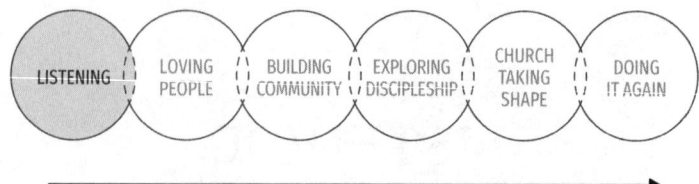

UNDERPINNED BY PRAYER AND CONTINUING CONNECTION TO THE WIDER CHURCH

It's generally unwise to set out on a journey without first studying the terrain you will be traveling and consulting the local experts. There's no shortage of such information available to help prepare for a thru-hike on the Appalachian Trail. From guidebooks to blogs to online forums, there are plenty of ways to research the route, plan supply drop offs, and buy the right gear. One of the most popular resources is the *Guthook* app for smartphones. Created by a thru-hiker, Guthook includes a compass, map, guidebook, and list of water sources along both the Appalachian Trail and the Pacific Crest Trail.[15] It's updated by crowdsourcing, making it the collected wisdom of thousands of thru-hikers, and access to this kind of information has revolutionized thru-hiking.

For better or worse, there is no *Guthook* app for understanding your community. You'll have to collect wisdom the old-fashioned way—knocking on doors, asking questions, and approaching your community as a learner.

Fresh expressions begin in a prolonged process of deep listening: listening to God and listening to your community. Your community is filled with local guides and helpful information. As you listen, you will look for where God is moving in the community. Tomáš Halík calls this process seeking *the*

---

15. Taylor Gee, "How the *Guthook* App Revolutionized Thru-Hiking," *Outside*, June 12, 2019, outsideonline.com/2396304/guthook-guides-app-mapping-thru-hiking.

hidden God—"the God whom we must seek and find in the lives of people beyond the visible boundaries of the Church."[16]

Be Opened

I remember my mom licking her finger and wiping food off my face as a child. Thinking about it still makes me squirm, but I do the same thing to my two-year-old daughter today. I cannot imagine doing it to anyone else, though. It's far too intimate and a little bit gross. Jesus never has been one for obeying our social norms though, has he? In one of those wonderfully odd Gospel stories demonstrating the closeness and intimacy with which the Son of God interacted with the hurting and suffering people around him, we see the following scene:

> [Some] people brought to him a man who was deaf and could hardly talk, and they begged Jesus to place his hand on him. After he took him aside, away from the crowd, Jesus put his fingers into the man's ears. Then he spit and touched the man's tongue. He looked up to heaven and with a deep sigh said to him, "*Ephphatha*!" (which means "Be opened!"). At this, the man's ears were opened, his tongue was loosened and he began to speak plainly. (Mark 7:32–35)

Ephphatha, pronounced "*ef-fath-ah,*" is one of the few words of Jesus that the Gospel writers chose to preserve in Aramaic. In doing this, they are highlighting something profound that was occurring—something significant enough to be tied to one of our most important church practices. In the

---

16. Tomáš Halík, *Night of the Confessor: Christian Faith in an Age of Uncertainty* (New York: Image Books, 2012), 46.

seventh century, the Rite of Ephphatha was part of a ceremony for converts that occurred the day before baptism. By the sixteenth century it was combined with the rest of the baptismal rite for adults and infants in the Roman Catholic Church, until the 1960s when it became optional.[17] It is profound that one of the first acts of becoming a disciple of Jesus is to have your ears opened. In the story, before the man could speak clearly, his ears needed to be opened. I know you are eager to proclaim the Good News of God's life-transforming love to your neighbors, but please first take the time for your ears to be opened.

Developing a Listening Ear

Adam McHugh writes, "Listening is a practice of focused attention. . . . In listening you center not only your ears but also your mind, heart and posture on someone or something other than yourself. It is a chosen obedience."[18] Before you go out into your community, practice listening in your home, in your close friendships, and at your workplace. Here are a few tips:

1. *Be curious.* Ask God for a generous helping of curiosity. Approach others as a learner. Every person you meet has something to show you about God, about life, and about the world. All you have to do is listen to them.
2. *Stop talking.* Our culture has put a high emphasis on having answers. Listening is about asking a good question and letting the other person talk. Ask questions that help you to understand the person in front of you.

---

17. Joseph A. Komonchak, "Ephphatha!" *Commonweal*, September 9, 2012, commonwealmagazine.org/ephphatha.
18. Adam S. McHugh, *The Listening Life: Embracing Attentiveness in a World of Distraction* (Downers Grove, IL: InterVarsity, 2015), 19.

3. *Give your full attention.* Jesus is remarkable at this. Rowan Williams noticed, "[Jesus] took it for granted that if there was somebody around, that somebody was worth his company—and that's how the church started."[19] Once someone starts talking, try to internalize what they are saying. If you feel your attention wandering, gently pull it back to the person in front of you.
4. *Stop making everything about you.* Resist relating what someone says to your own life. This one is hard. There might be a time for you to share with them that you have walked a similar path, but this is not the time.
5. *Don't give advice.* You might have a brilliant idea for how to fix all their problems. Save it for later. Jesus resists giving advice even when others are practically begging for it. He loves to answer a question with a question.

Listening Within Existing Relationships

Often a fresh expression will emerge from the interests and connections you already have. What are you passionate about? What aspects of life do you spend a significant amount of time thinking about? For instance, I'm fairly new to fatherhood. But while I've only been a dad for two years, it's now a central part of my identity. I think about it often, constantly wondering how I can be a better father. I also gravitate to other dads now, looking to learn and often commiserate a bit. In the UK, a popular fresh expression popping up is called "Who Let the Dads Out?" The first gathering began in a small Baptist church in Chester, and the movement has

---

19. Fresh Expressions, "The Archbishop and the Order of the Black Sheep," Fresh Expressions UK, YouTube video, 1:20, October 3, 2011, youtube.com/watch?v=8Jy7b-i_-bg.

grown to over 100 gatherings across the UK.[20] The name itself is just the right amount of cheesiness for dad humor—you can almost hear their kids groaning at the name. The gatherings bring together fathers and their children to have fun together and build relationships with other dads. What are important parts of who you are that could lead to a fresh expression like this? That is a great place to start listening. For my part, I can start talking to other dads at my neighborhood playground. I can reach out to a family-oriented non-profit in my town and see what they have learned about dads in our community. I can invite a few other dads from my church to help me get the idea off the ground. This is what it looks like to start with the interests and connections you already have.[21]

Listening Might Require Relocation

Listening might require you to physically put yourself in places you would otherwise not go, establishing what one scholar calls *an apologetic of presence*.[22] In 2017, we hired an intern at King Street Church who was interested in working with folks experiencing homelessness. For the first two months of his internship, Dustin spent his entire workweek listening. He began by looking for places where folks experiencing homelessness spent their time. He started with the homeless shelter, eating lunch there and sitting for hours in the foyer or parking lot and listening to as many folks as he could. He learned that many of the residents there would spend part of

---

20. Baptist Union of Great Britain, "Who Let the Dads Out," *Baptists Together*, January 1, 2020, baptist.org.uk/Groups/238638/Who_let_the.aspx.
21. For more see the "Love" section of the *Godsend* app on the "9. Innovate" page. The app is available at freshexpressions.org.uk/2018/12/27/growing-new-christian-communities-godsend.
22. Elaine L. Graham, *Apologetics Without Apology: Speaking of God in a World Troubled by Religion* (Eugene: Wipf and Stock, 2017), 127.

their day at the bus stop at Walmart. The bus stop had a covered bench and the businesses around didn't chase loiterers away. So Dustin started sitting at the bus stop for hours. It was often awkward, sometimes painfully so (one man asked him if he was a ghost!). Eventually, he formed relationships with the regulars. They started looking forward to their conversations with Dustin, even asking him to meet them there the next day when they saw him at the shelter. The bus stop became a field office of sorts for Dustin. His listening led to our fresh expression at the homeless shelter doubling in size.[23] We called him the King Street Church Minister of Loitering.

Simone Weil wrote that true attention is "the rarest and purest form of generosity."[24] If you want to serve your community, be attentive and listen with care. You might even learn to love it. One fresh expression leader told me of her process of drinking coffee and eating tacos with every community member she could find. Out of these listening sessions she discovered that many folks were interested in yoga. She's since trained to become a yoga teacher and started a yoga fresh expression that meets at a local business in town.

Many fresh expressions take on a "listening project," an intentionally devised and executed plan of listening to people in your community. First Canton United Methodist, a church of thirty-five in the hills of western North Carolina, knocked on the doors of 1,500 neighbors to ask how they could pray for them. They wrote down the answers, compiled the data, and were amazed at what they learned. Before the project began, members who had lived in Canton their

---

23. Dustin Mailman, "A Ministry of Loitering," *Fresh Expressions US*, March 27, 2018, freshexpressionsus.org/2018/03/27/a-ministry-of-loitering/.
24. Simone Pétrement, *Simone Weil: A Life*, trans. Raymond Rosenthal (New York: Pantheon, 1976).

whole lives said they knew all there was to know about their town. Yet none of them realized how many of their neighbors were mourning the loss of a loved one. As you listen to your neighbors, you are attending to Christ, in whom all things were created (Col. 1:14–23). First Canton now hopes to start a fresh expression for their neighbors who are in mourning.

As more of our social connections move online, listening online becomes more important. Try joining a local Facebook group, or a neighborhood app like *Nextdoor* or *Meetup.com* to see what you can learn about your community. In one community Facebook group that I'm a part of here in Charlotte, someone posted, "Name your hometown and state. Buffalo, NY, here." They received 590 replies! Some folks in the comments section discovered they had relocated from the same exit off the New Jersey Turnpike. Demographic mapping programs like MissionInsite can be super helpful too! There is a treasure trove of information about your neighbors and your neighborhood online if you know where to look.

Reading the Community like a Text

Listening to your community can be likened to deep reading. In both, we pore over what's in front of us as we look for its meaning. A few years back, I was invited to be part of a cohort of pastors involved in community engagement through the Lewis Leadership Center of Wesley Seminary. In the cohort, we were asked to read our community like a text. Think about the time and care that goes into reading Scripture. Preachers wrestle with passages all week. Some theologians wrestle with one passage their whole careers. This was how we were asked to look at our community.

As we read a passage, it's important to look to the cultural context—aspects of the author's culture that are foreign to our culture that influence the meaning behind the Scripture.

As you read your community, what aspects of the culture are going to be hard for you to understand? Who can explain them to you?

We also look to the historical context as we read a text. The Good News of Jesus is even better when we understand the oppression the Jewish people were enduring at the hands of Roman occupation at the time. When Jesus promises release for the captives, the original hearers understood this in ways that many of us today cannot fully comprehend (Luke 4:18). What is the history of the community you are listening to? It can tell you a great deal about its present situation. In a trip to Baltimore with the Lewis Center cohort, we learned about the history of "redlining," oppressive practices of the real estate industry that pushed people of color into the least valuable neighborhoods through selective raising of prices. The impact of the redlines of the 1930s can still be seen today.[25] Ignoring the history of your community leaves a giant blind spot in your understanding. Whom can you ask about the history of the community? Are there local historians, museum volunteers, archivists, or elderly residents full of stories? Is there an archive at the library, a local institution (like a museum or university), or a website that you can access? You might also look for someone who can give you the unauthorized history—the lesser told stories of the community, perhaps some of which the community has tried to forget.

Additionally, we often look to the original language to help with interpreting Scripture. There is a dizzying number of possible translations for each word in Hebrew and Greek, so Bible translators have to use context to make educated

---

25. Laura Bliss, "After Nearly a Century, Redlining Still Divides Baltimore," *Bloomberg Citylab*, April 30, 2015, citylab.com/equity/2015/04/after-nearly-a-century-redlining-still-divides-baltimore/391982/.

guesses on how exactly to translate these words. The community you are listening to has its own language, whether it is slang, spoken or unspoken, a mood, or a demeanor. In the North Carolina mountains they say, "I'm right smart with firewood," which means they have plenty. It's important to understand the language of the community you are listening to, not to inauthentically imitate it in an effort to fit in, but to understand the community better.

Lastly, we look to the interpretations of the text that others have made. We look to early interpretations of the church fathers and mothers and to more contemporary commentaries. These theologians offer us insight into the passage that we might have missed. Who are the expert interpreters in your community? These might be social workers, business owners, reporters, politicians, baristas, waitresses, or people "flying sign" on the corner asking for money. Artists, poets, and songwriters are great guides too. They make their living watching their surroundings, constantly looking for stories to tell. Charley Crocket on GemsOnVHS said, "Musicians are anthropologists. We study people and interpret [them]."[26] Whom can you ask for help in understanding your community? What questions should you ask them? If you fail to involve local leaders in your listening process, you are setting yourself up to start an unhealthy fresh expression. A slogan from the struggle of people with disabilities in South Africa sums it up well: "Nothing about us, without us, is for us."[27]

---

26. "Charley Crockett, 'Big Gold Mine,' //GemsOnVHS™," YouTube video, :20, July 23, 2018, youtube.com/watch?v=5BQEo5zXEBM&list=PLA42F6AB4204136B0&index=61.

27. James Charlton, *Nothing About Us Without Us: Disability Oppression and Empowerment* (Berkeley, CA: University of California, 2020), 3. Charlton notes that he first heard this slogan invoked by Michael Masutah and William Rowland, leaders of Disabled People South Africa in 1993. They had heard it used by someone at an international disability rights conference in Eastern Europe.

As we study and interpret the community, we understand our community more and more. And every piece of information we gather gives us a better chance of forming a fresh expression that will connect deeply with the people in our community.

JR Woodward gives four basic questions to ask to understand a particular neighborhood and/or city:

1. *Narrative*: What story is the city calling us to embody?
2. *Rituals*: What are the core practices people engage in that shape their identity and sense of mission in life?
3. *Institutions*: What are the primary institutions that are shaping the city, and how are they shaping people's identity and destiny?
4. *Ethics*: How would your neighborhood and/or city define success?[28]

Jon Davis, an Episcopal priest serving the Abbey Mission in Central Florida, reflects on how this process went for his congregation:

> God wanted to do something new and I needed to be still and listen, observe and discern what that new thing might be. I did not do this alone but invited members of the congregation to join me on Sunday afternoon prayer walks in the community. As we walked, we used all our senses to engage and understand. The questions we asked were: God, what are you already doing here, how are you already working? Who is here? What are the needs? How are we to make connections and

---

28. JR Woodward, "Exegeting a Neighborhood Within the City," *V3*, November 20, 2013, thev3movement.org/2013/11/20/exegeting-a-neighborhood-within-the-city/.

interact with the people in this landscape? A few things immediately happened. The locals who had lived there for decades began to see their community in a different light. They gained an understanding of the context, values, hopes and dreams of the people. God began to burden us for the people. It was less about doing something and more about being present with people.[29]

Whom can you invite to join you in this process of listening and learning? They might become fellow pilgrims on your fresh expressions journey.

Lectio Vicinitas

When I began thinking about reading my community like a text, I couldn't help but think about the process of *Lectio Divina*, the ancient monastic practice of prayerfully reading Scripture. *Lectio Divina* can be broken down into five movements or stages. I wondered if this practice could be applied to reading my community, and it worked remarkably well. I adapted the process to a community prayer walk and called it *Lectio Vicinitas*, or "Neighborhood Reading." It's designed to be done while walking through a neighborhood or driving through a rural community. I encourage church teams to practice this individually, and then compare experiences.

Amazing things happen when we open up our awareness to our neighborhoods. Without putting feet on the pavement, we miss everything. So lace up your prayer walking shoes and get out there!

---

29. Jon Davis, email message to author, October 7, 2020.

Lectio Vicinitas: Neighborhood Reading

1. Prepare *(Silencio)*
As you prepare to depart, quiet your inner voice. Invite the Holy Spirit to guide your steps and your observations. Seek a mindset of openness, leaving preconceived assumptions behind.

2. Read *(Lectio)*
As you begin walking, take special notice of whatever and whomever you see. In this stage try to minimize interpreting what you see and maximize observation. You can make notes on paper or on your phone if it helps you to remember. Take note of places where people are gathering. Look for written words on signs, posters, or magazines. Observe the housing in the community. If a property is for sale or rent, look up the cost. What stands out to you right away?

3. Meditate *(Meditatio)*
Find a quiet place to sit in the neighborhood. Reflect upon what you saw. Replay the walk in your imagination, stopping for moments that stood out to you. Ruminate on these moments. What stood out to you about them? Slowly shift your focus from the mind to the heart. What feelings were stirred in you? What was happening under the surface? Where did you feel God's presence on your walk? Where could you see God already working?

4. Pray *(Oratio)*
Shift into a conversation with God about what you saw on your walk. You can do this in a journal if it helps. Ask God some questions. Ask God for clarity in areas that are unclear. Ask where you might partner with God's redemptive work already happening in the community.

5. Contemplate *(Contemplatio)*
As you begin to close, jot down your newly discovered insights about your neighborhood. Write down anything you feel God was saying to you in this time. Rest in God's presence for a few moments before returning to your daily tasks.

Asking the Right Questions

Churches are notorious for starting a ministry without asking if the community wants or needs it. The listening stage is all about asking your community questions so you can understand it more deeply and form a fresh expression that is valuable and fits well within the community.

Not only is it important to ask gobs of questions, but it's equally important to ask the right questions as well. My wife is a physician assistant, and every time she sees a patient she asks a series of questions. If she doesn't ask the right questions, she can easily misdiagnose. As the inventor of the stethoscope said, "Listen to your patients. They're telling you how to heal them."[30] The point of my wife's questions is to determine the underlying causes of symptoms. This requires digging below the surface, seeing beyond the most obvious explanations. It's dangerous to treat symptoms without treating the underlying disease—you can't cure a brain tumor with Tylenol.

Jesus asks rich questions. Questions like, *What do you want me to do for you? Why this commotion and weeping? What is your name? Why are you thinking these things in your hearts? Do you believe this? Do you love me? What did you go out to the desert to see? Who do people say the Son of Man is? But who do you say that I am? What are you discussing as you walk along?*[31] One of my favorite questions he asks is, "How many loaves do you have?[32] Facing a hungry crowd with an obvious shortage of food, Jesus asks what they have, not what they need.

---

30. Michael Frost, "Listening Deeply to Your City," *Mike Frost*, February 16, 2017, mikefrost.net/listening-deeply-city/.
31. Charles Pope, "100 Questions Jesus Asked and You Ought to Answer," *Community in Mission Blog of the Archdiocese of Washington*, February 10, 2012, blog.adw.org/2012/02/100-questions-jesus-asked-and-you-ought-to-answer/.
32. Matthew 15:34.

This aligns with asset-based community development (ABCD), a strategy utilized by community organizers that emphasizes building upon the strengths of the community instead of trying to meet their needs with your resources. Instead of starting with needs, ABCD (and Jesus) starts with strengths. Here are some questions I have found to be helpful in listening to your community:

"Who is my neighbor?"

"What do my neighbors care about?"

"Where do my neighbors gather?"

"What activities are popular among my neighbors?"

"What do my neighbors think about faith and spirituality?"

"What gifts do my neighbors possess?"

"Who is isolated?"

"What burdens do my neighbors carry?"

"Who in my community is disconnected from church in its current form?"

"Where has Christ been ahead of me, planting seeds of Christian community?"[33]

---

33. For more questions see Michael Moynagh, *Being Church, Doing Life: Creating Gospel Communities Where Life Happens* (Oxford, England: Monarch Books, 2014), 165.

Approaching your community with rich questions that build on strengths will help you to understand the people among whom you are hoping to start a fresh expression of church.

Identifying Networks and Community Spaces

Growing up in western Massachusetts, my three best friends lived on the three streets closest to mine. We'd walk home from school together, ride our bikes around town, and stop at the Cumberland Farms gas station to buy gummy worms and Mountain Dew. With increases in social media use, mobility, and extracurricular activities, these kinds of neighborhood friendships are becoming foreign to rising generations. Increasingly, we relate most to those we share interests with, not those we live closest to. Ulrich Beck writes, "To live in one place no longer means to live together, and living together no longer means living in the same place."[34] We are increasingly connected by networks, not neighborhoods. Networks are the groups that people define as their communities (often found in leisure, work, and friendships). Your town has hundreds of networks like runners, gamers, retirees, and gym members. In a fresh expressions training I led in Georgia, a church leader said they had an Elvis impersonator conference in their town every year. Now that would make for an interesting fresh expression! As you walk through your listening process, make note of the networks you encounter. Begin to ask God if there is a network God is calling you to connect with.

Another important sociological concept to consider as you seek to start fresh expressions is shared community spaces, often referred to as *third places*. In response to a more digitally connected and yet more socially isolated

---

34. Ulrich Beck, *What Is Globalization?* (Cambridge: Polity, 2000), 74.

population, these community spaces are more important than ever, and they are quickly increasing in number. They are soccer fields, dog parks, barbershops, playgrounds, restaurants, gyms, comic book stores, and basketball courts, just to name a few. Ultimately, third places are "where everybody knows your name." For instance, Hooligans in Charlotte is a soccer-themed pub where fans go to watch English Premier League games with other fans. What are the shared community spaces you are encountering as you listen? Which ones stand out to you as potential places to start a fresh expression?

Don't neglect online networks and community spaces either! What are you passionate about? There's an online community for that. Whether it's Dungeons and Dragons players, bikers, bakers, runners, or dog owners, there's a Facebook group, a website, or an app connecting them. Many of these online spaces have geographical anchors too. "We Ride North Carolina" is a Facebook group for folks to find people nearby who ride motorcycles. "Moms of Huntersville NC" is a Facebook group in my town that has connected over 5,000 moms. In 2019 there were over 10 million Facebook groups and 1.4 billion people using them.[35] Head to facebook.com/groups/discover and browse the "popular near me" feed, or type your town or county in the search bar, and see what you can find.

Cultural Competency

Most fresh expressions will not be cross-cultural, but those that are will require plenty of time to listen to and find partners from that culture. Extra caution is needed in starting cross-racial fresh expressions—especially if you are coming

---

35. Christina Newberry, "33 Facebook Stats that Matter to Marketers in 2020," *Hootsuite*, November 24, 2019, blog.hootsuite.com/facebook-statistics/.

from a position of privilege. There is much history to be unpacked and much systemic racism that must be understood before such an endeavor can be made. In an essay that awakens the reader like a cup of ice water being splashed in your face, Christina Cleveland warns:

> Many urban church planters charge into cities with blatant disregard for the great ministry work that is already being done by under-resourced pastors and churches, blind to both their own privilege and their cultural incompetency and accompanied by the arrogant empire-based idea that more money means more effective ministry.[36]

And yet, God still calls some followers to cross cultures. If you think God might be calling you to cross cultures, it will require cultural intelligence and humility. Humility means recognizing that you are not anyone's savior. It means recognizing that the Holy Spirit has already been at work in the community long before you entered it. Your role is to point out where God has been at work and to help a community form around that. Humility also recognizes that you don't have all the answers. It requires you to lean on local wisdom and local leadership to shape the fresh expression. Lastly, humility means that you are looking for indigenous leaders to take more and more control of the fresh expression and for you to have less and less.

---

36. Christina Cleveland, "Are You Starting an Urban Church Plant or Plantation?" *Churchplants*, May 2, 2014, churchplants.com/articles/8449-are-you-starting-urban-church-plant-or-plantation-christena-cleveland.html.

Listening Leads Us to Our Who

The listening stage of our journey is not one to be rushed. A friend of mine took eight years to listen and form relationships with a group of youth in the trailer park where he lived before an opportunity for discipleship finally came around. He's an extreme case (then again, Jesus took thirty years to listen).[37] But the point is to wait for the Holy Spirit to lead. In our first fresh expression, King Street Church listened for three months before we were ready to move into the next stage. Be patient, savor every step of the journey, take in the beauty of the moment, and don't feel pressure to push your fresh expression to a step it's not ready for. That's the worst thing you can do.

On the other hand, listening ultimately leads to action. We listen so that we might obey the will of God when we eventually discern it. In Greek and Hebrew, the word for "listen" can also be translated as "obey." One writer says, "We listen as a sprinter in the blocks listens for the starter's pistol, muscles taut, poised for action."[38] Listening leads us to right action. We take our time, but eventually it's time to act.

The first action following listening is to begin to identify whom your fresh expression will connect with. They might be folks you already know or they might not be. You can't connect with everyone, so identify whom you will connect with first. This is the process of "defining your who." We do this by beginning to reflect on our emotions. Who keeps you up at night? Who stirs emotions of care and concern in you? In what places did you feel at home? In what places could

---

37. Michael Moynagh, *Being Church, Doing Life* (Oxford, England: Monarch Books, 2014), 164.
38. Adam McHugh, *The Listening Life* (Downers Grove, IL: InterVarsity Press, 2015), 72.

you see God clearly moving? Perhaps you can't stop thinking about the at-risk youth you encountered, perhaps you had some great conversations and felt at home at the neighborhood dog park, or perhaps your town's online poetry group has been a place where you've had a multitude of meaningful conversations. This may be the gentle pull of the Holy Spirit, calling you to a particular people or place.

In 2007, J.D. and Nicci Carabin drove by the skate park in Kalispell, Montana, and noticed a group of youth who were largely dismissed and forgotten. They began to bring the youth bottles of water and soon discovered that in the wintertime they had nowhere to skate. That winter J.D. and Nicci transformed their garage into a mini skate park, and Serious Ju Ju was born.[39] The group is now a Presbyterian worshiping community with a warehouse skate park and an appointed pastor who continues the work of creating a place for area youth to experience belonging and the love of God. In 2017, they baptized seventeen skateboarders and their friends and families.[40] Whom is God drawing you to?

---

39. Miriam Mauritzen, "Season 3, Episode 5: Miriam Mauritzen," *New Way*, January 20, 2020, audio, 4:00, newchurchnewway.org/podcast/home/2020/1/27/season-3-episode-miriam-mauritzen5.
40. Tom Esch, "Washed into Remission," *The Ministry Collaborative*, January 31, 2017, mministry.org/washed-into-remission/.

Further Reading:

Adam S. McHugh, *The Listening Life: Embracing Attentiveness in a World of Distraction* (Downers Grove, IL: IVP Books, 2015).

McHugh offers a comprehensive theological overview of listening. He argues that despite our current ineptitudes, we were created to listen.

Kate Murphy, *You're Not Listening: What You're Missing and Why It Matters* (New York: Celadon Books, 2020).

As a reporter for the *New York Times*, Murphy has mastered the art of listening. She brings together her experience and the expertise of people she has connected with over the years to take a captivating deep dive into listening.

Accompanying Prayer
A Collect for Listening

O Christ, who for thirty years listened in preparation for your ministry, attune our ears to the voices of our neighbors. Give us the heart to be captivated by the stories of our community, the attentiveness to be present in the spaces that matter to our neighbors, and the perceptiveness to see where you have already been at work. As we imagine how community can form around these things, let our listening cultivate the virtue of humility, for the vessel cannot be reshaped until it is emptied by our Potter, who reigns with thee and the Holy Spirit, one God, ever attentive. *Amen.*

— Terry Stokes

Chapter Three

LOVING PEOPLE

*"Friendship is the most important
sign of resurrection."*
— Fr. Juan Hernández Pico

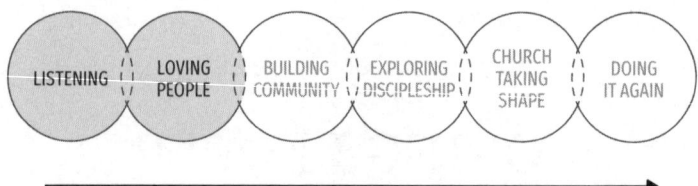

UNDERPINNED BY PRAYER AND CONTINUING CONNECTION TO THE WIDER CHURCH

When looking back upon a journey, it's the relationships that stand out. Thru-hikers often reflect on the importance of friendships along the Appalachian Trail. One hiker writes the following about completing the trail with her best friend and college roommate:

> When we were soaking wet from the rain, we'd sit together in our ponchos and listen to Hawaiian music, pretending we were on a warm and sunny island. When one of us fell down, we'd give the tumble a rating like we were judging an Olympic diving contest. When the only options you have are to laugh or cry, most of the time, it just seems better to choose laughter.[41]

The great Jesuit spiritual director William Barry asks, "What does God want in creating us?" He then answers, "God—out of an abundance of divine relational life, not any need for us—desires humans into existence for the sake of friendship."[42] Friendship is an outward expression of love. It is the essence of our relationship with God, and therefore

---

41. Heather Morris, "What It's Like to Hike 2,000+ Miles with Your Best Friend," *Shape*, February 28, 2020, shape.com/lifestyle/mind-and-body/hiking-appalachian-trail-with-best-friend.
42. William A. Barry, *A Friendship like No Other: Experiencing God's Amazing Embrace* (Chicago: Loyola Press, 2008), xiv.

friendship is the basic building block of church.[43] We cannot have a church without friendship.

As the process of starting a fresh expression progresses, leaders must look for opportunities to love others and see how the Holy Spirit might deepen existing relationships and generate new ones with people outside of the church. In one of the most widely quoted verses of the New Testament, John 3:16, we are told that Christ's journey toward us is rooted in love.[44] Therefore, our fresh expressions journey must also be rooted in love. To move forward in the journey for any reason other than love would be to risk manipulation. It's important to remember that you are forming friendships simply to enjoy a relationship with your neighbors. Whether these friendships lead to a fresh expression is up to the Holy Spirit.

A Loving-First Journey

In one of the many tense scenes between Jesus and religious leaders in the Gospels, we see an expert of the law test Jesus:

> "Teacher, which is the greatest commandment in the Law?" Jesus replied: "'Love the Lord your God with all your heart and with all your soul and with all your mind.' This is the first and greatest commandment. And the second is like it: 'Love your neighbor as yourself.' All the Law and the Prophets hang on these two commandments."[45]

---

43. See John 15:14–15.
44. Dave Male, *How to Pioneer* (London: Church House Publishing, 2016), 41.
45. Matthew 22:36–40.

We must ask ourselves, "Is my fresh expressions journey rooted in these two commandments?"[46] If it's not, you will need to press pause and get your intentions right. A fresh expression rooted in love seeks justice for the oppressed, welcomes in the stranger and the outcast, and always widens the circle of belonging a little more. This basis in love is so important to the process that the fresh expressions journey is now widely referred to as a "loving-first journey."

The creators of the *Godsend* app, a helpful resource for starting fresh expressions, warn, "Beware of rushing in to build community and sharing faith with people. You can only really build community with people and share faith with them if you have loved them first. . . . To really make a difference we need to have meaningful relationships."[47] To truly love someone, you must release your expectations and enjoy the person for who they are. Take time to savor relationships; don't use your friends to populate a preconceived program. There may come a time when you will be invited to share your faith with your friend because they ask you. Or there may be a time when you can invite them into your fresh expression that is forming (or they might invite themselves). They might even create a fresh expression with you. But that time may never come. The people you meet may simply be new friends to enjoy. Being open to that possibility will keep you from being manipulative. Don't be surprised if you are invited into their lives also! As we formed King Street Church, I never turned down an invite to an underground hardcore

---

46. For more see Michael Moynagh and Michael Beck, *The 21st Century Christian: Following Jesus Where Life Happens* (Richmond, VA: Fresh Expressions US, 2020).
47. Fresh Expressions Resourcing, "Loving Ideas Video" *Church Support Hub*, October 25, 2018, churchsupporthub.org/godsend/stage-2-love/loving-ideas/.

punk show. Believe it or not, I was always the only minister in attendance.

Tim was one of our first members of King Street Church. He eased into our community warily because he carried a great deal of pain from past experiences with Christianity. A few years before, he had started attending a campus ministry where everyone was kind and welcoming. He had never been a part of a faith community before, and he grew closer to God in this loving community. But when he had a period of doubts that wouldn't go away, his friends started acting differently. When he ultimately made the decision not to be a Christian, his friends staged an intervention. When it failed to change his mind, they stopped inviting him to hang out. He was devastated because he realized his friendships were built on conditions, and when he didn't conform to their conditions, the friendships were over. This realization pushed him away from the church. We must be better than this! We must love without conditions.

Finding Early Partners

The fresh expressions journey is moving toward building a community, and in order to build a community, you will need some help. As you spend time investing in relationships, who stands out to you as a potential partner in starting a fresh expression? In Luke 10, Jesus gives us a framework for finding such partners. When Jesus sends out the disciples, he instructs them to eat and drink with those who welcome them, and then proclaim that the kingdom of God is near. He says, "When you enter a house, first say, 'Peace to this house.' If someone who promotes peace is there, your peace will rest on them; if not, it will return to you."[48] A person who "promotes

---

48. Luke 10:5–6.

peace" is someone who resonates with your vision and welcomes you into their life. This is who Mike Breen calls a "person of peace."[49] As your vision for a fresh expression starts to take shape, it's time to start looking for persons of peace who can join you on the journey to God's kingdom and help you navigate the path forward.[50]

When King Street Church was just an idea floating around in my head, I started asking folks I knew for recommendations of whom I should talk to about starting a Christian community in downtown Boone. Someone said, "You need to talk to Elizabeth, she's like the mayor down there." Elizabeth, a refugee from fundamentalism, had been attending the contemporary service at Boone UMC sporadically over the past year. I asked her to meet me for coffee at Espresso News, a little coffee shop off of King Street with a mean light roast. As I tried to share my dreams for a new Christian community in downtown Boone, we must have been interrupted a dozen times by people Elizabeth knew. She would ask each person a personal question: "How is your mom doing? Did you get that job? Are you feeling any better?" I later found out that some of the folks downtown called her "The Boone Angel" because she was always around and ready to be a support. After all of the interruptions, I knew I wanted to start a fresh expression of church with her. Elizabeth brought to our budding fresh expression a decade of relationship building with the downtown community, her outgoing personality that never hesitated to invite new folks in, and her gift of hospitality that welcomed our ragtag group

---

49. Mike Breen, *Building a Discipling Culture: How to Release a Missional Movement by Discipling People like Jesus Did* (Greenville, SC: 3DM Publishing, 2017), 116.

50. For an excellent overview of this concept, see Michael Moynagh, *Church in Life: Innovation, Mission, and Ecclesiology* (Eugene: Cascade Books, 2018), 41–44.

into her home for casseroles each week. Her stamp of approval for our burgeoning group gave us instant rapport among the people with whom we wanted to start a fresh expression. She quickly became our King Street Church mom. Elizabeth and I were totally opposite, but we made a perfect team. I wanted things to be more churchy, and she wanted things to be way less churchy. I am fairly reserved and conflict avoidant, and she would not hesitate to tell me something was "bulls**t." Yet every time we disagreed about something, we found a middle ground that worked. After seeing her name in Travis Collins's book about fresh expressions, Elizabeth thought it was hilarious that she was called a person of peace. I replied, "You certainly are a particularly aggressive person of peace."

Focus on Relationships

So how do we find early partners? We pray. Then we focus on relationships. As mentioned in the last chapter, these might be existing friendships or they might be new ones. As you spend time listening within your existing relationships, ask yourself what friendships you can invest in. Could these connections be the start of a fresh expression? Perhaps you're an artist and you know a few other artists. Focus on deepening these relationships, and also think about how you might expand your network. Even if you know plenty of people, it will be important to get out there and get to know new people.

One attendee at a recent Fresh Expressions event reflected, "How do you find these people? My days of being plugged into the community are long passed!" She represents many of us in the church who will need to spend a bit more time making connections in the community before moving forward in the journey. Perhaps you are new to a community, or perhaps all of your friends are already a part of your church (or another church in town). It's never too late to reconnect to the community outside of the church. Where have you been connected before? Perhaps you used to be involved at the local school but lost touch when life became too busy. Or perhaps you used to be a regular at the local gym when you took a weekly class there. You might be able to jump right back in where you left off.

The only way to form relationships with those outside of the church is to go to where the people are and to invite them into your life. How does Jesus meet new people? Jesus goes to where the people are, he attends parties, talks to strangers, goes to their places of work, goes to the well (the Judean version of a coffee shop), is a dinner guest at others' homes, goes for walks, visits the marginalized, performs miracles, and heals others—just to name a few. Imagine that, right there in front of us in the Gospels, is a guide for loving people and building new relationships that can lead to Christian community. Granted, we might not be able to summon up miracles quite so easily, but don't underestimate the restorative power of relationships.

We form friendships with others when we inhabit the same spaces they do. Jason Byassee calls it "loitering with intent."[51] Entering space that is not your own requires humility, and there are some spaces that are not open to visitors, so be discerning. However, if you spend all of your time in the church, all of your friends will be in the church. If you're going to start a fresh expression, that has to change.

Here are a few ideas for deepening existing relationships and forming new ones:

Go for Walks. It's good for you and it's good for starting fresh expressions. You can listen to the community as you

---

51. Jason Byassee, *Northern Lights: Resurrecting Church in North England* (Eugene: Cascade Books, 2020), 24.

walk, pray for people when you walk by houses, pray for businesses, and depending on the culture of where you live, you can start having conversations with the people you see. If you walk regularly, you might see the same person over and over and a conversation might end up happening naturally. The first few conversations might revolve around the weather or dog breeds, but it won't take long to find new and deeper conversation topics.

Become a Regular. Another great way to develop friendships is to become a regular at a community space. As you listen to the community and begin to identify shared community spaces, maybe one will stand out to you. David Fitch was walking in a Chicago suburb when he saw four men talking in a bar. He recognized the desire he saw in their eyes as a desire for communion with Christ. Since then he's become a regular there, going every week on the same night to talk to others, occasionally having opportunities to share his faith.[52] What shared community space draws you? Start going regularly and have conversations with others. Maybe there's a local gym you can go to every Monday after work. Maybe it's a coffee shop you can answer emails at on Wednesday mornings. Maybe there's a dog park around the corner that you can go to every Saturday. Be brave, talk to new people, introduce yourself to others, talk to your waiter or bartender (if it's slow), ask people questions. And the most important thing—keep going back. You'll know you have arrived when they know what you're going to order as soon as you walk in: "You want your usual?"

---

52. Paul J. Pastor, "David Fitch: Recognizing Christ's Presence—Part 1," *Outreach*, April 2, 2018, outreachmagazine.com/interviews/27716-david-fitch-recognizing-christs-presence-part-1.html.

Be a Good Neighbor. Just because our culture's social dynamics are changing doesn't mean we should not look to our immediate neighborhoods as a place to start fresh expressions. Bishop Ken Carter writes, "If we focus solely on neighborhoods, we will miss the reality of communal networks; but if we don't seek to preserve the strengths of neighborhoods, we won't offer an alternative to the individualism that pervades our culture."[53] Whether it's by baking cookies or hosting a block party, find a way to meet your neighbors. Our subdivision's HOA invites a food truck to set up by the neighborhood playground every Friday evening. It's been a perfect way to get to know our neighbors (and our local food scene). One activity you might try is drawing a map of your immediate neighborhood and filling it out with the names of your neighbors. See how many neighbors you can invite over for dinner in the coming year. Even if this doesn't lead to a fresh expression, it's an important part of being a disciple of Jesus.

Digital Connections. If we are to go to the people, we cannot ignore where people spend a massive amount of their time: online. One thing the COVID-19 pandemic has taught us is the gift of digital relationships. We are able to connect and share our lives with people across vast distances. And yet social distancing also taught us the limits of digital relationships. There is something significant about flesh. In Christ, even God has flesh. There is a genuine need for in-real-life (IRL) friendships. In the digital age we have incredible social tools at our fingertips, but the trick is to use them in a way that doesn't eclipse IRL friendships. For instance, digital relationships can lead to IRL friendships. Two of my coworkers love Dungeons and Dragons (D&D), and as their D&D

---

53. Kenneth H. Carter and Audrey Warren, *Fresh Expressions: A New Kind of Methodist Church for People Not in Church* (Nashville: Abingdon Press, 2017), 55.

group was dissolving, they turned to the "Looking for Players and Groups" board on dndbeyond.com. The forum has over 15,000 threads of people looking for groups to join. They quickly found five people in the Charlotte area who were interested. They had their first meeting on Zoom—to make sure no one gave off the axe murderer vibe—and then started meeting in the side room at a local comic book store. Websites that are dedicated to a particular affinity group are abundant, as are sites like *Meetup.com* that offer a platform for everyone from poets to hikers to blue grass musicians.

Connect in Networks. It's easier to develop friendships with folks with whom you share an interest. As you listened to your community, did you encounter people you could relate to? Our postmodern society can be understood as a giant web of networks. We interact most with the people in our networks, which are based on shared interests and shared experiences. This can be a career, a hobby, a medical diagnosis, a focus on social justice, a cultural background, or an area of study among many others. Is there a network that you are interested in? People love that Frederick Buechner quote, "The place God calls you to is the place where your deep gladness and the world's deep hunger meet."[54] I always laugh when someone mentions it to me. What does it say about my gifts and passions that I started a church in a bar? I guess it's like that country song "I'm Pretty Good at Drinking Beer."

Eat Together. If you were looking for Jesus during his earthly ministry, more likely than not you would have found him at the table. Like the Very Hungry Caterpillar, he ate his way through the Gospels. Sitting down to eat with people was essential to his earthly ministry, and it is equally essential

---

54. Frederick Buechner, *Wishful Thinking: A Theological ABC* (London: Collins, 1973), 95.

to ours. The first four months of King Street Church were purely focused on sharing meals with people we met in the community. We hosted potlucks, but there are many ways to do this. Some people are comfortable inviting people over and cooking for them. Some are more comfortable ordering takeout and watching a football game. Others are far more comfortable inviting people to go out to lunch or breakfast and let someone else do the cooking and the dishes. Kendall Vanderslice observes, "When Jesus established his church, he did so around the table. He asked his followers to eat together in remembrance of him, knowing that the process of sharing a meal communicates something vital about who we are and how we relate to God."[55] There is no better place to spend your time starting a fresh expression than around the table.

Be a Guest. There's another way to build relationships that's closely related to the last one. Be a guest. In the Gospels, Jesus went to weddings and always accepted an invite to a good party. For this he was accused of being a glutton and a drunkard (Matt. 11:19). My favorite way he was a guest is when he literally invited himself over for dinner. He said, "Zacchaeus, come down immediately. I must stay at your house today."[56] There's a defensiveness in American Christians that often keeps us from accepting hospitality from others. We feel like we should be the ones hosting them. But accepting someone else's offer of hospitality is the most empowering act we can do. If you are willing to host someone, but unwilling to be their guest, it's a sign you see them as lesser. Where can you be a guest? Where can you invite yourself over? What public events (online or in-person) can you attend? For example, Simple Church, a dinner church in Massachusetts, rents

---

55. Kendall Vanderslice, *We Will Feast: Rethinking Dinner, Worship, and the Community of God* (Grand Rapids: Eerdmans, 2019), 168.
56. Luke 19:5.

a booth to sell bread at the local farmer's market. Simple Church finds the market is a fundraiser for their budget, but even more it's a way to meet new people and invite them to check out their dinner church. Let someone else plan the party; just show up and focus on building friendships.

Serve Others. Finally, another way to develop relationships is to find ways to be helpful to others. Early on, the Fresh Expressions movement in the UK heavily emphasized this concept. In fact, this whole stage of the fresh expressions journey was once called "Loving and Serving," and the entire process in the UK was called a "serving-first journey." However, I am wary of this approach in the United States. I think it is a dangerous language for our charity-soaked church culture that is obsessed with measurable success. The predominant form of service in the American church is an industrialized charity marred by savior complexes, where you can almost see the capes church people are wearing. I speak so passionately about this because I have lived it.

This kind of service is a lousy foundation for community. The giver/receiver dynamic is difficult to break. Andy Milne points out, "This stage [of the fresh expressions journey] is about building relationships of trust and respect with key people in [your] context."[57] Charity is perhaps the worst way to build relationships of trust and respect. It's important to keep in mind that as you form friendships, you will want to do it in a way that leads to community. American forms of service are far too intertwined with our work ethic that looks at the world (and others) as problems that need to be fixed. Not only is this a false reading of social problems, it's also

---

57. Andy Milne, *The DNA of Pioneer Ministry* (London: SCM Press, 2016), 54.

dehumanizing and just plain bad theology. People can't be flipped like houses.[58]

Every Monday night for four years, I ate dinner at the local homeless shelter and hosted a fresh expression with the residents after dinner. Each week I walked through the buffet line, receiving the meal from volunteers from area churches. I'm pretty sure half of the church ladies in Boone think I am homeless. One week I went through the line, thanking each person for the food they placed on my tray. An elderly volunteer turned to another and said, "Wow, he is so polite." It was as if she perceived the invisible wall between the haves and have-nots and thought it was soundproof. There is no potential for a meaningful relationship to form when there is an invisible barrier separating you from the other person.

There is a way of serving others that is mutualistic and builds healthy relationships. John Perkins points out that Jesus asked others for help. By asking the Samaritan woman for a drink of water, Jesus "demonstrated she had something of value that she could share with him—Jesus affirmed her dignity and broke down the wall of distrust."[59] Fred Rogers, patron saint of neighborliness, was known to ask people he met to pray for *him*. When visiting a boy with cerebral palsy, he asked the boy to pray for him, and the boy's mother cited this moment as a turning point in her son's mental health and self-confidence.[60]

---

58. Erin Tatum, "Why Your Savior Complex Is Toxic to Your Relationship," *Everyday Feminism*, October 13, 2014, everydayfeminism.com/2014/10/savior-complex-toxic-relationship/.

59. John Perkins, *Beyond Charity: The Call to Christian Community Development* (Grand Rapids: Baker Books, 2004), 33.

60. Tom Junod, "Can You Say . . . Hero," *Esquire*, April 6, 2017, esquire.com/entertainment/tv/a27134/can-you-say-hero-esq1198/.

Chuck and Elissa Huffstetler are starting a fresh expression in their neighborhood of primarily international refugees in Charlotte, North Carolina. Chuck has made it known that he's happy to help neighbors haul things in his pickup and help the neighborhood kids fix their bicycles. But Chuck also knows that he can ask these same neighbors for help when he needs it, and when he broke his leg that's exactly what he did. His next-door neighbor started pulling his trash can in on trash day and told Chuck he was praying for him every day. These mutual acts of service form bonds and strengthen relationships. This is neighborly service. You do something nice for your neighbor, and in turn you ask your neighbor for help when you need it. This is a great way to start a fresh expression.

If you are stuck in a giver/receiver dynamic, you can change it. Angelica Regalado Cieza, a Moravian minister in Winston Salem, North Carolina, founded Estamos Unidos, a fresh expression that offers educational opportunities and faith formation for immigrants. She found that the shift from service to community occurred when she started doing home visits with families. She remarked, "When people share a living room or a table, the conversations flow more naturally, different types of conversation occur, not just about education, but about family, and about our immigration stories. And it's not just one way, it's not just me helping them, it's them knowing me, and me knowing them."

Conclusion

Forming friendships is a lot like dating. I realized this when my family moved last year. As soon as we moved the first box into our new house, my wife was on the prowl for mom friends. To see her at work was like watching an expert pickup artist. Every time we would go to the neighborhood playground, she would leave with the digits of another mom and plans for a playdate in the works. She'd get extra nervous about how she worded her first text messages to them. In a scene straight out of a Lifetime movie, she met her new best friend at the local farmer's market. If you've spent any time dating, you know it's full of contradictions. It's terrifying and exhilarating, fun and depressing, draining and life-giving. It often feels easier to just give up. If you're feeling like your days of being plugged into the community are long passed, don't give up. Get back out there and make some new friends.

Further Reading:

William A. Barry, *A Friendship like No Other: Experiencing God's Amazing Embrace* (Chicago: Loyola Press, 2008).

Barry is a Jesuit spiritual director, so prepare your spirit to be filled with a desire for a closer relationship with God. It's a short, beautiful read about friendship rooted in God.

Kat Vellos, *We Should Get Together: The Secret to Cultivating Better Friendships* (self-pub., 2020).

Vellos has written a fun and brilliant handbook for forming friendships in our over-worked, hyper-transient, and digitally consumed world. It's written with young, urban populations in mind, but everyone will learn from her advice on how to rise above the challenges of making friends.

Accompanying Prayer
A Collect for Loving People

O Christ, you began your earthly ministry by making friends, and your ministry consisted largely of making new friends. As we do the same, lead us to the spaces where we can know and be known, help and be helped—never in a hurry, never with conditions, always open to whatever the Spirit has in mind to create, who reigns with you and our Friend, in triune community. *Amen.*

— Terry Stokes

Chapter Four

BUILDING COMMUNITY

"Nobody talks about Jesus' miracle of having 12 close friends in his 30s."
— @mormonger

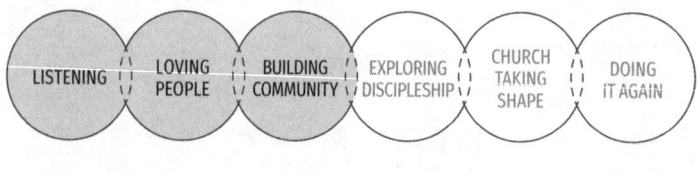

UNDERPINNED BY PRAYER AND CONTINUING CONNECTION TO THE WIDER CHURCH

Journeys bring people together. Thru-hikers on the Appalachian Trail often settle into a *tramily* (trail family). These small groups of hikers tend to share a similar pace and ideological approach to hiking. They keep each other company and encourage one another as they walk from Georgia to Maine. Paty, trail name *SISU*, a veteran of the US Army and thru-hiker, wrote,

> Choosing one's tramily is more than merely happenstance though. You can hike around someone for days or weeks and not become anything more than acquaintances. The people who ultimately become your tramily are the ones who share your values and goals. They belong in that small group you want beside you during the inevitable ups and downs. They are the friends who make your hike more vibrant, and those people you will tell stories about long after you're off the trail.[61]

As you listen to your neighborhood and begin to form new relationships with those in your community, you will begin to identify a group of people you can invite to form a new community with you: your very own *tramily*.

---

61. Paty Matiskella, "Friends & Tramily," *Outdoor Pilgrim*, September 27, 2019, outdoorpilgrim.com/friends-tramily/.

Fresh expressions differ from many other church planting models by creating a social community before creating a spiritual community. As you deepen existing relationships and form new ones, it's often too soon to invite your friend into a spiritual community. Give the relationship time to deepen and grow. And there's no better place for relationships to grow than in community.

A Place to Belong

In an age of increased digital connectedness, Americans are experiencing loneliness—the pain of feeling disconnected—in epidemic proportions.[62] Loneliness is a result of too few meaningful social interactions. In Cigna's *2020 Loneliness Report*, 61 percent of respondents replied that they are lonely.[63] When we look to the earthly ministry of Jesus, we see him constantly creating meaningful social connections. Jesus was magnetic, and the community surrounding him must have been too. It just kept growing and growing as the excluded found a place to belong. At one point, the church knew how to create meaningful social interactions too. We knew how to throw a mean party. Rodney Stark writes of the early church,

> Christianity revitalized life in Greco-Roman cities by providing new norms and new kinds of social relationships able to cope with many urgent urban problems. . . . To cities filled with newcomers and strangers, Christianity offered an immediate basis

---

62. Frank J. Ninivaggi, "Loneliness: A New Epidemic in the USA," *Psychology Today*, February 12, 2019, psychologytoday.com/us/blog/envy/201902/loneliness-new-epidemic-in-the-usa.
63. "Loneliness and the Workplace," *Cigna*, January 23, 2020, cigna.com/static/www-cigna-com/docs/about-us/newsroom/studies-and-reports/combatting-loneliness/cigna-2020-loneliness-infographic.pdf.

> for attachments. To cities filled with orphans and
> widows, Christianity provided a new and expanded
> sense of family. To cities torn by violent ethnic strife,
> Christianity offered a new basis for social solidarity.[64]

Building community was the best play in our playbook, and we let it slip away.

Feelings of loneliness point to the instinctual desire for community. We are created in the image of God, and therefore the desire for community is imprinted upon us. God exists forever in the perfect Triune community, and remarkably, we are invited into this community. On the night of Jesus' arrest, he prays, "My prayer is not for them alone. I pray also for those who will believe in me through their message, that all of them may be one, Father, just as you are in me and I am in you. May they also be in us so that the world may believe that you have sent me."[65]

This is the invitation of Christian community: to be one with one another, and one with God. And to invite our neighbors in too! If you have experienced such a community, you know how beautiful this can be (its messiness notwithstanding).

Communities begin with gathering people together. Whether online or in-person, every time you gather is another step toward a cohesive community. Each gathering will shape the identity of the budding community, so designing our gatherings should be done with care and intentionality. Let's walk through planning your first gatherings.

---

64. Rodney Stark, *The Rise of Christianity: How the Obscure, Marginal Jesus Movement Became the Dominant Religious Force in the Western World in a Few Centuries* (New York: HarperOne, 1997), 161.
65. John 17:20–21.

Chapter Four | Building Community

Whom Will It Bring Together?

Revisiting a question from the listening stage, whom do you feel called to bring together? At King Street Church, our *who* changed over the six years I was its pastor. At first, we primarily connected with young people who spent their time in the coffee shop by day and underground hardcore punk music shows by night. Later, our tendency toward radical acceptance connected us with men in the county jail, and we were able to walk with them as they navigated release from incarceration and entry into new life. Take some time to reflect upon the people you have met and the friendships you have formed. With whom did you feel a deep connection? What group of people do you sense the Holy Spirit might be calling you to form a community with? Now is a good time to invest some serious time and energy into prayer. Approach God with these questions and ask trusted friends to join you in praying for the Spirit's guidance.

One more thing about your *who*: remember, fresh expressions exist for the benefit of those not already connected to the church. I have had countless conversations over the years with people starting fresh expressions who are only connecting with church people. This almost always means they haven't spent enough time in the first three steps of the journey. Don't dismiss the possibility that you might need to ask church people to stay away for a while as you begin your fresh expression. Church people love new and shiny ministries and won't hesitate to "come check out what you are doing." Yet their presence will change the atmosphere of your gathering and influence the community identity that is still forming. Too many church people will quickly make it another church function—just a more fun one. It's okay to ask church folks to give you some space and visit later on.

Why Are You Gathering?

Before you gather, it's also important to explore the simple question: Why are we gathering? Perhaps you are gathering to offer support to single mothers, to create a place for storytellers to share their stories with each other, or to create a safe space for people in mourning to process their grief. The community's purpose should be developed with the people you are gathering and should be something the group commits to working on together.

Francisco Garcia-Velasquez is a Methodist minister in Chula Vista, California. After facing a devastating tragedy, he found that hardcore punk music (similar to heavy metal) had an ability to heal him in ways that nothing else did, even his Christian faith. The rawness, the honesty, and the communal expression of emotion were medicinal for him.

This intersection of faith and hardcore punk stuck with him. In his first church appointment out of seminary, Francisco began to learn about his congregation and about the surrounding community. Much to his delight, he discovered a thriving local punk scene. He started attending shows, going to local record shops, and meeting folks who shared his love for punk music. As he formed relationships, he realized that the San Diego area was lacking safe venues for hardcore punk shows. He and his new friends, including local bands like Take Offense, PSO, and Nerve Control, began to explore what it would look like to create a new venue in town.

He asked his church if they would help. The church secured a location, and local punk bands came together to renovate the property. The venue began hosting bands like Turnstile, Terror, and Power Trip. Pretty soon, First United Methodist Chula Vista had hardcore punk on Saturdays and handbells on Sundays. Francisco knew the power of hardcore punk music, and he knew the power of Jesus. He wanted others to find the healing and sense of belonging he had discovered in both. He invited others into forming the venue and the community within it, and this is why it was wildly successful in connecting with those outside of the church. You can read more about him by running a web search for "Moshing with Methodists."

> Our Vision: "Our community brings together _____ so that we can _____."
> (who) (why)

Source: Bailey Richardson, Kevin Huynh, and Kai Elmer Sotto, *Get Together: How to Build a Community with Your People* (San Francisco: Stripe Press, 2019), 31.

How Will You Gather?

Your purpose should drive how you gather. Many fresh expressions gather around a common interest. For example, one fresh expression in Florida gathers movie lovers once a month to attend a movie together, and then they head to a restaurant after for a conversation about how the movie speaks to their lives. A fresh expression in North Carolina gathers older adults who are looking to become more physically active. They gather every week for a group exercise class.

You've made connections with lots of different people. Of those most hungry for community, what kind of gathering would they come to? A jog, a meal, a server on the *Discord* app, a conversation over coffee, lawn chairs pulled together at the dog park, a Zoom conversation? Include your people in the planning and implementation of the gathering. Share the load and spread out the ownership.

One Time or Regular?

There are two types of gatherings that are important to the formation of a community: one-time events and regular gatherings. One-time events increase the number of people in your fresh expression's social circle and help you form valuable community partnerships, whereas a regular gathering is about building consistent, lasting community. If you're starting a fresh expression with runners, you might host a 5k charity fundraiser as a one-time event and start a weekly group run as your regular gathering.

Ahmani Pegues graduated from college with a degree in public health and moved back to her hometown of Hickory, North Carolina. Her grandparents had passed away and left her family a house in a neighborhood of the city that she knew had higher than average rates of preventable disease. She decided to start a community wellness house, a fresh expression designed to educate the surrounding community around health and wellness and introduce faith. In order to start forming community, she invited neighbors to community garden workdays as well as one-time events like "As a Black Man" and "As a Black Woman," where they discussed issues of physical and spiritual health and self-care. This is exactly what we are hoping for in one-time events: Ahmani met folks from the neighborhood and began to build relationships with local agencies that focused on public health in Hickory. Unfortunately, Ahmani was not able to get the support she needed to keep the project going. Reflecting on the importance of continuous community engagement, she said, "A project or initiative will not survive if community members do not work collaboratively."⁶⁶ The fresh expressions journey is all about exploration and experimentation. Not every idea will become a fresh expression and that's okay. We'll dive deeper into this in Chapter 8.

One-time events are important, but community forms in consistent gatherings. Regular gatherings can be monthly or weekly. Include your people in shaping the gathering. At the first gathering of our poetry fresh expression at King Street Church, everyone in attendance shared our hopes for the group and discussed the order of future gatherings. We brainstormed a list of potential activities we could do together and after some conversation landed on a basic order. Don't hesitate to make changes to your gathering as it moves forward. See what works and what doesn't. Seek feedback from your people as you grow. If people come back, ask them what they like about the group and how you can make the group better. If people come only once, follow up with them and ask them why they didn't come back. Use this feedback to improve the gathering. To keep momentum going, agree on a date for your next gathering before your time together is over. "This has been fun. When should we get together again?" If people are willing, get their contact information so you can send them a reminder.

Where Should We Meet?

A Baptist lay person started a fresh expression with bikers in Virginia where they sip whiskey and smoke cigars while discussing life and faith in his semi-finished barn. Sign me up! The rustic, rough-hewn setting is perfect for a bunch of men sharing about their rough-hewn lives. A fresh expression in Florida meets at the community dog park. Several of our rural

---

66. Ahmani Pegues, Facebook message to author, November 24, 2020.

fresh expressions in western North Carolina have met at volunteer fire departments, which have a community room that can be reserved. These are just a few of the places fresh expressions meet—the possibilities are endless.

The church has grown far too comfortable in church buildings and is missing opportunities to gather in public places. Meeting in public is more work than reserving a room at the church, but it opens your fresh expression up to all kinds of people who wouldn't enter a church. It can also put you out in plain view of your community, giving people an opportunity to wander up to your gathering and ask, "What are you all up to?" The location of your gathering also shows your identity to the community and differentiates your group from people's past experiences with church. I can't tell you how many times someone has commented about King Street Church, "I don't go to church, but I would try a church that met in a bar."

I am often asked how to go about starting a gathering in a public place like a pub. If you are gathering in a way that does not differentiate you from typical patrons (e.g., normal group size and everyone is buying something), I don't typically see a need to ask for permission right away. However, if the group starts to grow, if the group acts differently than the rest of the patrons, or if you are advertising your gathering in any way, then I would approach the owner. You can expect the owner to say something along the lines of, "As long as you're buying our products and as long as you're not scaring away our other customers, come on." One owner asked that we not take up all his parking spots. The owner of the Boone Saloon asked us to meet on a slow night of the week. Boone Saloon filled up every week for Taco Tuesday, but Sunday nights, when we met, were usually pretty dead. Communicate regularly with the owner and tip your waiters and bartenders as if they were

Jesus himself, and they'll be happy to see you come back. You might be surprised; the owner might start sending people to your fresh expression or join it themselves!

You can build community online too. Interactive apps and websites like Facebook Groups, Discord, Geneva Chat, and Slack have the ability to create meaningful community among people online in addition to in-person gatherings.

Nathan Webb is a pastor and self-proclaimed nerd and gamer. Nathan's church uses *Twitch*, a streaming platform, for reaching out to new people and leading conversations about recently released games and all kinds of other nerdy topics. These streams can have as many as 450 people watching and participating. From there, he looks to connect his new friends into the church *Discord*, a community platform and app—what he calls "our virtual church building." Currently there are about thirty active members of the church *Discord*. Nathan is quick to point out that building relationships is essential to every online ministry.[67] As with in-person gatherings, give your members opportunities to interact with each other directly—don't feel the need always to intervene or mediate.

When Should We Gather?

As with other areas of planning, when you gather will depend on who is coming together. Sarah Watkins Davis is a deacon at a church in Gastonia, North Carolina. Her church engaged in a listening project where they prayer walked a quarter mile radius around their church. As they walked the neighborhood, they realized that the vast majority of their neighbors were businesses that were occupied from 9–5 p.m.

---

67. "Gaming Church," *Field Preachers*, audio, soundcloud.com/field-preachers/field-preachers-episode-62-gaming-church.

Their church programming, including their dinner church, happened from 6–8 p.m. When they shifted dinner church to lunch, they saw a huge increase in attendance from local business folks. Prayer has a way of opening our eyes and increasing our awareness of the Spirit's nudging. Experiment with different times and poll the people you are hoping will join. You can even use an online tool like doodlepoll.com, which allows you to suggest various times and see what works for the most people.

Make It Participatory

A thriving community is participatory. Look for ways to create an engaging dialogue among the group. Rotate the responsibility of leading the gathering every week. Assign roles to group members based on their gifts. If someone is a good communicator, ask them to send out invitations. If someone is extroverted, ask them to keep an eye out for visitors and talk to them. If someone is social media savvy, ask them to update the Twitter and Instagram accounts regularly. If someone has the gift of hospitality, ask them to host the group for dinner every so often. The more evenly the responsibilities are spread across the group, the healthier your fresh expression will be. As Peter writes, "Each of you should use whatever gift you have received to serve others, as faithful stewards of God's grace in its various forms."[68] Lead your fresh expression like that!

Make It Fun!

When immersed in solemn forms of gathering, we church types can forget that the foundation of our faith is rooted in delight. Not only does Jesus throw a good party, he brings the

---

68. 1 Peter 4:10.

good wine. And if it runs out, he makes more! Joy and laughter draw people into a community like nothing else.

Steve North, a pastor in Toledo, Ohio, encountered a group of starving artists in his city. He loved getting to know them and started inviting them to his house for dinner. The dinner went so well they kept offering it, and the gathering became a fresh expression called Lifeline Toledo. Their monthly community dinners are known throughout the city for their eclectic crowd and for lasting late into the night, usually wrapping up around 2:30 a.m.[69] Steve knows how to throw a great party!

At King Street Church, we were always looking for an excuse to throw a party. We celebrated after a baptism, we celebrated birthdays, we celebrated graduations, and we celebrated when our church members finished out parole without recidivating. Sometimes I wonder how much of our church decline is due to boredom. Perhaps in church we feel a need for all of our gatherings to be filled with solemn spiritual content, and we forget that laughter and delight are vital for any community. Maybe that's why several successful mainline church plants are led by former stand-up comics.[70]

How Big?

Bigger is not always better. The Jewish concept of the *minyan* is helpful when thinking about the size of fresh expressions. *Minyan* is a quorum of ten adults required for public worship and is still present in much of Judaism. Its origins are

---

69. "Community Dinners," *Lifeline Toledo*, accessed June 24, 2020, lifelinetoledo.com/community/community-dinners.html.
70. See Jason Byassee, "Cutting-Edge Orthodoxy," *Sojourners*, April 2014, sojo.net/magazine/april-2014/cutting-edge-orthodoxy, and "Professional Comic Turned Preacher: Rev. Jerry Herships," *UMC* (February 2015), umc.org/en/content/professional-comic-turned-preacher.

found in the story of Sodom in Genesis 18, where Abraham convinces God to spare Sodom if ten righteous men can be found there. Brian Sanders observes that the *Minyan* shows us that in God's eyes, ten people is enough to save a whole city.[71] The average size of a fresh expression in the UK is forty-three, and the vast majority of fresh expressions gather ten to fifty people.[72] This is counterintuitive to our megachurch culture. In Chapter 6 we'll discuss how creating multiple small fresh expressions can impact as many or more people than a warehouse full of worshipers.

Getting People to Show Up

Are you starting to picture what your gathering might look like? Now, I bet you're wondering how to get people to show up. It's simple: invite people you've already formed a relationship with. Save your mass marketing budget and use it for beer money. In all seriousness, mass marketing should be of little importance to a fresh expression because you're building a community with friends you've met earlier in the journey. Marketing for a one-time event can be an exception because these are designed to increase the number of people in your social circle, but otherwise you won't have much use for it.

While mass marketing is unhelpful, intentionality in your invitation is essential. For example, Blake Trent is a pastor in North Georgia who started Wing Church, a fresh expression that gathers at a local pub's wing night. Every week he uses a wing-related meme for his Facebook invite. It communicates the time and location, but it also paints the gathering as

---

71. Brian Sanders, "The Power of 10," *Medium*, March 24, 2019, medium.com/@BSunderground/the-power-of-10-878b01034238.
72. Sabrina Müller, "Fresh Expressions of Church and the Mixed Economy," *International Review of Mission*, November 7, 2019, doi.org/10.1111/irom.12282.

something fun and enjoyable. Priya Parker suggests that the tone and style of your invitation is as important as the information within it. She remarks, "An invitation is a priming device, a psychological invitation to say, 'On this future date, for a specific moment in time, for this purpose, I'm going to be creating this temporary alternative world. Won't you join me in helping build it?'"[73]

Invitations remain important throughout the life of your fresh expression. Sending weekly reminders with the who, what, where, when, and why of events will keep you on the forefront of your people's busy minds and schedules. A group text is easy but has the potential of becoming annoying if it gets used too much. Apps like *Slack*, *Whatsapp*, and *Discord* might be a better bet.

As your community grows and matures, inviting new people into it remains vital. If your fresh expression stops bringing in new people, it has started to die. Howard Thurman writes, "Community cannot feed for long on itself; it can only flourish where always the boundaries are giving way to the coming of others from beyond them."[74] New people bring much-needed energy and vibrancy, and it's important that your members have a shared responsibility to bring new folks in. Everyone in your group has friends they can invite. Your job is to make the gathering worth sharing and make sharing easier for them. The authors of *Get Together*, my favorite book on building community, point out, "Once members know that they play a role in attracting new folks, your next

---

73. Priya Parker, "How Is This Night Different Than All Other Nights?" *Together Apart*, April 8, 2020, audio, 4:20, podcasts.apple.com/us/podcast/together-apart/id1506057555?i=1000470869135&fbclid=IwAR0w5dy3qji_iv74_-fZiYGYuxx-14jKXZWdI6eI7zY6rWZRvDN66JVxQxGs.
74. Howard Thurman, *The Search for Common Ground* (New York: Harper & Row, 1971), 104.

step is to make sharing easy, even exciting, for them. Serve up the rad photos, videos, or language they'll be excited to use when they tell friends about the community they're a part of."[75] Another way to grow your community is to utilize two to three people excited about the gathering whom you ask to invite others. For example, Daniel was a manager at a local hotel. When he came to our fresh expression at the Boone Saloon, he loved it and started inviting everyone he knew. Pretty soon half of the people in our gathering were people he worked with at the hotel.

Getting People to Come Back

Get Together highlights another important lesson: "Regardless of what drives people to show up for the first time, the relationships they form are what will bring them back. Meaningful human connections are sticky."[76] What can you do to increase the chances of people interacting with each other during the gathering and afterwards? Leave room for conversations; help people who are shy meet others by introducing them and helping them start conversations with others. "Hey, Tori, this is Henry. Y'all both love Beyoncé." Take a bow and back away.

Some of the most successful communities I've witnessed start to use the language of "family." It's quite fitting, as the early church gathered as an *oikos*, meaning "household" or "extended family." The New Testament regularly uses the language of sister and brother, which may sound cheesy to us now, but shows that family was reordered around Jesus Christ. How can you make your community feel like a family? When new folks feel like they belong, they will come back.

---

75. Richardson, Huynh, and Sotto, *Get Together*, 74.
76. Ibid., 55.

Establishing a Group Identity

As your group continues to gather, a group identity will emerge. You can help shape this identity by establishing rituals, badges, and a shared language.[77] A ritual is something that brings the group from one state of mind into another. Try to establish a beginning ritual and ending ritual for the gathering. Be creative! If your group is gathering single moms to de-stress and support each other, you might begin the gathering with a collective sigh. Many fresh expressions begin gatherings with "highs and lows," where everyone shares the best moment and the hardest moment of their week. Try to end the gathering with intentionality too. Keep it simple at first. Once you introduce a faith component to your gathering, you can start to add some rituals from the church's rich liturgical tradition.

A badge is anything visual that marks affiliation with a group. At King Street Church we had a tattoo artist friend make us a simple logo that we could print on stickers. I paid him in PBR pints at the Saloon. When one of our couples was pregnant, we threw them a baby shower at the pub. Along with a bunch of diapers, we gave them a onesie with the logo. Not only was it ridiculously cute, but it showed the parents that their little baby was part of our family. If you don't know a tattoo artist, check out fiverr.com for freelancers who can create something for you at an affordable price.

Developing a language of your own can be a marker of belonging. Just be careful that it doesn't isolate visitors. For example, F3 is a nationwide, faith-based men's workout group that functions much like a massive network of fresh expressions. At the end of your first visit they assign you a nickname.

---

77. Ibid., 91.

Like a trail name on the Appalachian Trail, it's your identity in the group from that point forward. Mine is "Barbless," after my love of fly fishing. After such an intense workout, I was just glad they didn't call me "Breathless." Eventually, your group can have its own demonym. No, not a demon. A demonym is a word that identifies a group of people from a particular place, such as New Yorkers or Chicagoans. At King Street Church we called ourselves King Streeters—not all that clever, but the more we used it, the more united we felt.

Establishing a Group Covenant

At some point it will be important to formalize group expectations. Your first big conflict is a perfect time for you as the leader to ask the group to establish a covenant, or a set of ground rules for the gathering. A covenant identifies what the fresh expression is about and how people are expected to participate within it. Try to make it somewhat light and fun, lest the group feel like they're in school or therapy. One of our rules at King Street Church was, "Jesus paid for your sins, not your beer, so don't forget to close your tab." Establish a group covenant that you can fit onto a sheet of paper and give to everyone who comes. It will be a good reminder for your regulars and helpful for new folks too.

Porous Borders

Idealists will want to create a community for everyone (I know because I am one). In reality, there is always some sort of border around a community—that's what makes it a community. The trick is making it the right kind of border. I like to think of a cell membrane that lets the right things in quickly but keeps things out that will harm it. We need to keep certain things out of our community; the question is how to do that without becoming closed off. Honestly, this is a balance I never truly figured out with our fresh expressions that emphasized radical inclusion. Several of the fresh expressions I started ended because one or two toxic people drove them into the ground. I appreciate Dave Andrew's community rule: "Bizarre behavior is okay. Abusive behavior is not okay."[78] You might have folks join your community who are awkward or who struggle communicating with others. As a leader, it's your job to step in and help them. Abusive behavior is anything aggressive, coercive, manipulative, or destructive. If someone acts abusive, there must be immediate consequences. As a leader, pull them to the side and tell them why their actions were inappropriate and that there is no room for that in the group. If things don't change, or abusive behavior becomes a pattern, you might need to ask them not to come back. If possible, see if you can connect them with a community that might be a better fit for them. This is never easy, but sometimes necessary, and having these tough conversations can be easier if you invite your leadership team to help.

Forming a Team

As your community forms, it will be important to share responsibility and control of the group by creating a leadership team.[79] Two or three people is usually perfect, but larger fresh expressions might require more. The people on your leadership team are the ones you will pray with on a regular basis and make important decisions with. In Jesus' missionary strategy in Luke 10, he sends the Seventy out in pairs, a strategy that continues in the book of Acts with Paul and

---

78. Craig Greenfield, *Subversive Jesus: An Adventure in Justice, Mercy, and Faithfulness in a Broken World* (Grand Rapids: Zondervan, 2016), 56.
79. For more thoughts on team development in a fresh expression, see Michael Moynagh, *Being Church, Doing Life* (Oxford, England: Monarch Books, 2014), 157–160.

Barnabas and in the Letter to the Romans with Andronicus and Junia (Rom. 16:7). Jesus knew that apostolic ministry was not meant to be done alone.

Calvary Baptist Church in Bowling Green, Virginia, is launching multiple fresh expressions in a rural county. They started an outreach in a trailer park, a recovery group, a stretching and nutrition class, and an art class. While each of these efforts is still in development, what's beautiful about their fresh expressions team is the way they care for and complement each other. Each member of the team is the lead on one of the projects and plays supporting roles in the other projects.

Online communities require a team as well. They often include three roles: *Platform owners* or *platform stewards* set the rules for the community. *Super participants* are the most active contributors to the community who create, edit, organize, and moderate the content that makes up the community. Lastly, *participants* are the everyday community members who consume, share, and adapt the content of the community.[80] Everyone has a role!

Facebook Groups Are Real Communities

Do not underestimate the power of creating an online community! In an interview on the *Get Together* podcast, Lindsay Russell, a former marketing manager at Facebook, tells the story of one member of "Girls Love Travel," a Facebook group dedicated to solo female travel. The member was solo-traveling in Thailand, had a medical issue, and needed emergency surgery. She posted about it on the group's page. When she

---

80. Jeremy Heimans and Henry Timms, *New Power: How Power Works in Our Hyperconnected World—and How to Make It Work for You* (New York: Anchor Books, 2019), 88–89.

woke up from surgery, two members of the Facebook group were sitting by her bedside.[81] These are real communities!

Missing Peace, a worshiping community in Ormond, Florida, engages their Facebook group with regular video messages, virtual service projects, mindfulness moments at home (cooking, surfing, doodle art, poetry, etc.), and content related to what is going on in the world. They even hosted a "Photographathon," a virtual family photo challenge event.[82]

In the podcast episode mentioned above, Russell highlights five of the most important characteristics of meaningful Facebook communities:

> *Identity*: The group provides a strong sense of identity.
>
> *Usefulness*: The group fulfills a real need.
>
> *Voice*: Members of the group feel like their voice matters.
>
> *Distinct Culture*: The group forms traditions, norms, hashtags, and its own language.
>
> *Sense of Safety*: The group creates and enforces guidelines that provide psychological safety for its members.

Keep these things in mind if you are considering starting an online community, and be sure to visit some popular online communities to see how they do it. Russell speaks

---

81. "What Makes a Facebook Group 'Off the Charts' Active with Lindsay Russell, Facebook," *Get Together*, audio, 50:40, podcasts.apple.com/us/podcast/get-together/id1447445682?i=1000486978171.
82. "Missing Peace," Facebook, accessed September 12, 2020, facebook.com/groups/291694061410772.

highly of "Dogspotting," a community of 1.8 million members dedicated to the lifestyle of spotting random dogs.[83]

Conclusion

Forming community is what the church is called to do. *The Book of Common Prayer* declares, "The mission of the Church is to restore all people to unity with God and each other in Christ."[84] In other words, the church can be understood as a community gathered by Christ to be part of his body.

This chapter is packed with directions and might have you feeling like this is going to be too much work. In truth, a great deal of this stuff is going to happen naturally. If you're sharing leadership responsibility, it won't feel like work. In fact, it should be incredibly life-giving to be a part of community like this. After hiking with a tramily, hiking alone just isn't the same.

---

83. "Dogspotting," Facebook, August 1, 2020, facebook.com/groups/dogspotting/.
84. *The Book of Common Prayer: And Administration of the Sacraments and Other Rites and Ceremonies of the Church* (New York: Church Pub., 2007), 855.

Further Reading:

Charles E. Moore, Called to Community: The Life Jesus Wants for His People (Walden, NY: Plough, 2016).

Moore has compiled an epic anthology of readings on Christian community. Be warned: the authors are committed to the radical call of the gospel as it relates to living together. It's convicting, to say the least.

Bailey Richardson, Kevin Huynh, and Kai Elmer Sotto, *Get Together: How to Build a Community with Your People* (San Francisco: Stripe Press, 2019).

It's hard to put into words how much I love this book. It's a fun, simple, and compelling manual for creating communities in the digital age. The authors lead an organization called People & Company that helps organizations create authentic communities. Be sure to check out their podcast too!

Accompanying Prayer
A Collect for Building Community

O Holy Spirit, you came with power upon the new community that Jesus had founded and anointed it as the church. Do the same for the new fellowships we build, that they too might become a source of belonging, identity, and purpose. Add group culture to our interlocking friendships, that we might become a structure whose significance and staying power exceeds any one iteration of our group. And make our alternative world come more and more to resemble the new reality that is breaking in by the power of our Father who reigns with you and our Savior Jesus Christ, one God, in glory everlasting. *Amen.*

— Terry Stokes

Chapter Five

EXPLORING DISCIPLESHIP

*"If you make disciples, you always get the church.
But if you make a church, you rarely get disciples."*
— Mike Breen

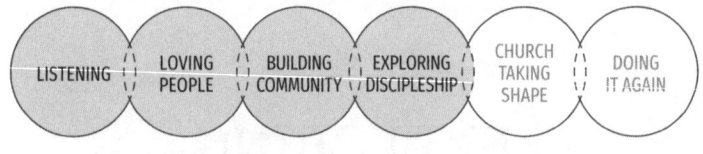

UNDERPINNED BY PRAYER AND CONTINUING CONNECTION TO THE WIDER CHURCH

Warren Doyle has hiked the Appalachian Trail eighteen times. And yet his legacy lies in the wisdom he has passed on to countless other thru-hikers. In 1989, he founded the Appalachian Trail Institute, a five-day course that covers trip logistics, physical conditioning, and the psychological demands of long-distance hiking. In addition to classes, students go on afternoon "diagnostic hikes."[85] Doyle has also accompanied eight groups of hikers the length of the trail since 1975. Participants in Doyle's guided hikes are required to attend sixteen days of intensive preparation and pledge to finish the trail as a group unless there's an emergency.[86] Each year less than 25 percent of thru-hikers complete the Appalachian Trail. However, 75 percent of the graduates of Doyle's five-day course completed it, and seven out of eight of his guided trips had a 100 percent success rate.[87] Doyle has created a system that combines classroom learning, apprenticeship, and commitment to the group, and it has been wildly successful. In fresh expressions, we must do the same.

Inviting someone on a journey of faith in Christ without preparing them for the challenges ahead does not give them

---

85. "Appalachian Trail Institute," *Warren Doyle*, accessed March 22, 2020, warrendoyle.com/ati.
86. "The 2017 Appalachian Trail Expedition," *Warren Doyle*, accessed June 22, 2020, static1.squarespace.com/static/56a590ee1a5203313c-3859be/t/56a7d527a976afe7fc4d821f/1453839655766/2017+Exp+INFO.pdf.
87. Ibid.

a very good chance of success. Teaching the ways of Christ and applying them to real-life examples in an hour on Sunday morning is better. But the surest way to success is a combination of classroom teaching, practical preparation, and walking alongside them as they grow in Christ. In close community we can show others the pace, point out the hazards along the way, and surround them with a community of fellow pilgrims committed to picking each other up when we stumble.

Formal and Informal Discipleship

The Greek word for "disciple" is *mathetes*, which translates as "learner." To become a disciple of Jesus means to become a learner of Jesus, and as we learn from Jesus we begin to live like him. A disciple of Jesus seeks closeness with God, loves their enemies, lifts up the downtrodden, doesn't grasp for worldly power, and turns the other cheek.

There are two approaches to learning the ways of Jesus: formal discipleship and informal discipleship. Formal discipleship is the learning that occurs from reading, listening to others, and participating in planned discussions. When I learned to fly fish in college, I read every book by Tom Rosenbauer I could find, watched YouTube videos until my eyes hurt, and took a fly fishing class at Appalachian State (yes, we have the best P.E. classes around!). In fresh expressions, formal discipleship is almost always conversational. A group of people from the fresh expression who are interested in discipleship will gather to discuss a passage of Scripture or a particular aspect of following Jesus.

Informal discipleship is the learning that occurs in everyday life. While my fly fishing studies were helpful that year, the most important learning came from time on the Watauga River with my friend Vern. Vern showed me how to fish in *our rivers*. Many of the tips in books didn't apply to our area—styles of casting meant for wide open rivers out West were not practical for our narrow streams with trees hanging over them. This informal learning alongside a trusted mentor was vital to mastering my new obsession.

Whether it's resolving an argument in the group or processing a traumatic event in your town, in informal discipleship every situation and experience become an opportunity to learn about following Jesus. Monica Coleman writes,

> My daughter's infancy is teaching me about faith formation. . . . Her inability to speak elaborate language or complex argument reminds me that my own formation wasn't verbal. It involved my grandmother preparing Communion wafers, the sounds of Negro spirituals, the songs of Vacation Bible School. I want my child to know about Christianity, but I want her to love God and church more. I want to put our faith in her heart and her bones.[88]

In fresh expressions, discipleship is happening all the time. If you are a leader, you are teaching others how to follow Jesus not only in your formal gathering but also with your every word and action (no pressure!).

Opt-In Discipleship

In a fresh expression, discipleship begins with opting in. For it to be any other way would be manipulation. Jesus let the rich ruler walk away. He also said to "shake the dust off your feet" in response to rejection—that is, respect the word "no."[89] Once you have built a community, you will prayerfully wait

---

88. Monica A. Coleman, "Follow Me," *Monica A. Coleman*, August 1, 2013, monicaacoleman.com/follow-me/.
89. Matthew 10:14.

Chapter Five | Exploring Discipleship

for opportunities to invite members of your fresh expression into a discipleship journey. Your job as a leader is to look for those in the group who are ready. When you have identified them, here are a few ways to invite folks to opt in to discipleship:

Have a set time of transitioning from fellowship to discipleship: Dinner churches often utilize this one. The dinner church begins with a meal, and at a set time the gathering transitions to a time of discipleship. Some utilize a little sign on the table that says, "If you'd like to stick around after the meal, at 6:15 we will be sharing a short story about Jesus and praying for everyone who is present." This gives people an opportunity to slip out if they are not interested. The loud and chaotic atmosphere of dinner church means slipping out isn't awkward or even very noticeable. Verlon Fosner, pastor of a multi-site Assemblies of God dinner church in Seattle, tells the story of a middle-aged man who attended their dinner church in the Greenwood neighborhood:

> He was a friendly guy and really enjoyed the good food and the laughter around the table. But whenever I arose to start the Christ story, his countenance would darken, and he would walk out of the room. When the preaching was done, he would come back in, grab another plate, and resume with the table life and laughter. Often as he was leaving, he'd say to me, "If you guys don't stop with that Jesus stuff, this dinner will die—people won't put up with this." Well we didn't stop, and it kept growing until the room was filled beyond capacity.
>
> One evening I grabbed my plate of food and sat down next to him and learned that both of his teenage kids

> had been murdered on the same night by gang members some years earlier. That event thrust him into the good/evil paradox—if God is good, how could he let this evil thing happen? I was broken-hearted as I listened to his pain; I understood why he couldn't stay in the room and listen to us talk about a God whom he held such anger for. From then on, whenever I was about to start the Christ story, I would go to Don, tap him on the shoulder, and quietly tell him to go out for a smoke break because I was about to start. He was surprised the first time I did that. I bet he genuinely appreciated my care for him. After a few months, I noticed that he stopped leaving the room when I preached. And after a couple more months he started looking up from his food during the Christ story and actively listened. And a couple months more he started to visibly engage in our prayer times. His heart was being healed before our eyes.[90]

Verlon made it clear that discipleship was this man's choice, and that participation in it was by no means a condition of belonging.

Transition from one space to another: At Snow Hill UMC in Candler, North Carolina, they host a flea market in the church parking lot every Saturday morning. While the flea market is happening, they host a short breakfast church in the fellowship hall. The flea market carries on and attendance at the breakfast church is completely optional.

One-on-one transition: You might find that in your budding community only one person in the group is ready to begin the journey of discipleship. Start meeting with them

---

90. Verlon Fosner, email message to author, October 27, 2020.

Chapter Five | Exploring Discipleship

for coffee or lunch and see what happens. After a while, you might be able to invite another person, and then another.

Start an additional gathering: One of my favorite fresh expression pioneers, Andy Milne, describes the discipleship stage of his fresh expressions journey with at-risk youth in Bradford, UK: "This stage started for Sorted because we wanted to take a smaller number from our big gathering and discuss faith in God using the Bible and praying together, just as Jesus preached to the gathered crowds and then went deeper with a smaller number of disciples."[91]

At Sorted, this meant that their Friday evening dinner and skateboarding with at-risk youth remained unchanged. But on Wednesday they invited the youth to come discuss a story about Jesus and then skate. While Friday might have one hundred youth, Wednesday only had twenty, but it was twenty youth with no other church connection, beginning their walk with Christ. What I love about this strategy is that it leaves the original gathering unchanged. By not messing with the social gathering, you are leaving the front door of your fresh expression wide open for new folks to keep entering in.

Full group transition: In some instances, the whole community is interested and willing to introduce an element of discipleship. This was how we introduced discipleship into our first fresh expression at King Street Church. One important lesson we learned the hard way was that we ended up accidentally closing the front door of King Street Church. As the group grew in discipleship, we stopped hosting our potlucks, which had been an easy space to invite new people into our fresh expression. We slowly stopped adding new people to our fresh expression, and this presented problems further down the line. If your whole group decides to transition into

---

91. Andy Milne, *The DNA of Pioneer Ministry* (London: SCM Press, 2016), 55.

discipleship, you will need to find other ways to invite new people in.

Spiritual from the start: Some fresh expressions find it easier to have a spiritual element from the very beginning. As your group is forming in the building community stage, you invite people into a community that will be exploring spirituality and faith together. In other words, you combine the third and fourth stage of the journey. This can work well, especially if you have built deep friendships in the second stage.

Kris Beckert, a Nazarene minister, leads a hiking fresh expression called "Happy Trails." In the group, about half are Christian and half are not. She begins each hike with a Scripture reading, a short reflection, and a question to discuss together as they hike. At a recent hike, Kris read from Ecclesiastes, "Whoever watches the wind will not plant; whoever looks at the clouds will not reap."[92] The conditions that day were rainy as she talked about how we often wait for the perfect conditions to make a decision in our lives. Group members reflected on their experiences with this in the past. As they began hiking, Kris posed the question, "As we're hiking today in these imperfect conditions, think about a situation where you have been waiting for the perfect conditions and ask if God might be calling you to move forward." Folks who are not Christian know that the hike will open with Scripture, but the conversation is presented in a way that they feel welcomed and free to be themselves. Many of our neighbors outside the church are eager to talk about life and faith in a setting that encourages exploration and respectful disagreement.

Discipleship hub: I've seen this one a few times. A church that starts multiple social gatherings can host one discipleship

---

92. Ecclesiastes 11:4.

gathering that the others feed into. For example, one multicultural church in Charlotte has a community garden and a Hispanic youth soccer league that have introduced them to countless neighbors. Out of these relationships they had a huge pool of friends to invite to their bilingual dinner church. Of course, not all of them came, but many did!

An existing ministry becomes a fresh expression: What ministries at your church have formed a community of folks otherwise disconnected from church? You might already have a ministry that can very easily become a fresh expression. A feeding ministry that has built relationships with community members could become a dinner church. A youth basketball league could spin off a fresh expression. A church-based preschool could start a Messy Church.[93] There might be low-hanging fruit in your church!

Creating the Right Environment for Discipleship to Occur

I've tried to keep a fish tank a few times in my life. Every time it has ended in disaster. I changed out dirty water or I introduced a new fish causing some aspect of the water quality to go wrong, and all the fish end up flushed. A fresh expression's environment is just as finicky. When entering into discipleship with folks who deeply distrust the church, all they need is one reason to not come back. One inappropriate comment, one correction about a personal belief they hold, or one judgmental look is all it takes. Creating the right environment takes care and intentionality. People need to feel safe and welcome.

---

93. For more ideas about adapting existing ministries, download the *Godsend* app available at freshexpressions.org.uk/2018/12/27/growing-new-christian-communities-godsend/.

One aspect of a hospitable discipleship environment is attentiveness to language. The shared language of the group should prioritize those who are not Christians. This means avoiding "Christianese," those phrases that people outside the church have no way of understanding. In addition, group leaders should encourage "I" language. For example, "*I* believe that prayer draws us closer to God" is far better than "Prayer draws us closer to God." Or worse, "As we can all agree, prayer draws us closer to God." There can be no assumption of shared beliefs in a fresh expression. Everyone will be in a different stage of their faith journey, and "I" statements clarify that this is okay, and in fact, a good thing.

If you want discipleship to occur, you also need vulnerability. If you want to kill vulnerability in a group, offer unsolicited advice. Nearly every Christian group I have ever been a part of has had a well-intentioned member who was quick to reply to others' vulnerable disclosures of personal pain with shallow and thoroughly unhelpful advice. Nip that in the bud right away. Make it clear that group members should only give advice when they are asked for it, and perhaps resist even then! Emphasizing confidentiality at every gathering is important too. Private thoughts shared in the group should not be repeated outside the group. Confidentiality is an essential ingredient of trust.

Discipleship Pathway

In order to guide someone along the discipleship journey, it's helpful to have a map. In church we often call this a discipleship pathway—a series of programs or resources available to new people to help them mark progress in discipleship. The problem is most discipleship pathways start (and finish!) with someone showing up on Sunday morning and the church assimilating them into church life. While this pathway may be true discipleship for some, about 60 percent of the US population is alienated by prevailing forms of church and will not be coming to us at all.[94] We need a pathway that starts long before Sunday morning, one that is situated in everyday life.[95]

Don Everts and Doug Shaupp interviewed 2,000 young people who had come to faith in Christ in Southern California. Here are the steps of the path that they found:

Step 1	Trusting a Christian	"Some Christians are okay."
Step 2	Becoming curious	"Jesus is interesting."
Step 3	Opening up to change	"Jesus could be for me."
Step 4	Seeking after God	"Jesus is worth taking seriously."
Step 5	Entering the kingdom	"I'll turn to Jesus."
Step 6	Living in the kingdom	"Help me to live like Jesus."
Step 7	Inviting others to join	"My friends should know Jesus too."

Source: Don Everts and Doug Shaupp, *Pathway to Jesus: Crossing the Thresholds of Faith* (Nottingham: Inter-Varsity, 2009).[96]

As we consider inviting our friends into this sacred journey, it's helpful to have this pathway in mind. If we can

---

94. Alan Hirsch and Dave Ferguson, *On the Verge: A Journey into the Apostolic Future of the Church* (Grand Rapids: Zondervan, 2011), 29.
95. Müller, "Fresh Expressions of Church and the Mixed Economy."
96. I first encountered a version of this in Michael Moynagh, *Being Church, Doing Life: Creating Gospel Communities Where Life Happens* (Oxford, England: Monarch Books, 2014), 144. It was adapted slightly from Don Everts and Doug Shaupp, *Pathway to Jesus: Crossing the Thresholds of Faith* (Nottingham: Inter-Varsity, 2009). I've also adapted it, using their alternative threshold descriptions, and adding the final step. Note: the updated title of this book is *I Once Was Lost: What Postmodern Skeptics Taught Us About Their Path to Jesus*.

identify where they are in the journey, we will know how to walk alongside them in their pilgrimage. Instead of looking at our friends as people who hold status as a non-Christian or a Christian, it's far more helpful to view all of us as pilgrims on the journey to following Christ, each with multiple thresholds to cross, only rarely aware when we have done so.

Before we explore each of these stages, it's important to remember that everyone takes this journey at a different pace. Our job is not to shove the pilgrim forward, but rather to be careful observers, constantly looking for the moment the Holy Spirit is inviting the pilgrim into the next leg of the journey. Our role is to be a guide pointing out the next stretch of the trail. Rowan Williams describes the patient discipleship of Jesus,

> Looking once again at the Gospels it seems pretty clear that Jesus expects some people to change pretty quickly and yet he sits in those long, patient meandering conversations—with the Samaritan woman at the well, and Nicodemus—as if to say, "Alright so you haven't got it yet. Let's keep at it and don't be rushed," and I think that is how Jesus relates now to people.[97]

Few of us will experience a fast conversion like Paul. Far more of us will experience the gradual conversion of inheriting the faith from a trusted friend or family member like Timothy did.[98]

---

97. Rowan Williams, "Making the Mixed Economy Work," *Dr. Rowan Williams 104th Archbishop of Canterbury*, May 6, 2011, aoc2013.brix.fatbeehive.com/articles.php/2044/making-the-mixed-economy-work.
98. See 2 Timothy 1:5.

Trusting a Christian: "Christians are okay."

Our neighbors have a long list of good reasons to distrust Christians. Shoot, I'm a pastor and I distrust Christians. We're the worst. When you encounter people out in the community, you start at a disadvantage. You unwittingly trigger their past experiences with Christians. Whether they've been yelled at by a street corner preacher or have more personal negative experiences with the church, Christianity carries very few positive connotations for many in today's world. When non-Christians aged sixteen to twenty-nine years old were asked about their current perception of Christianity, 87 percent responded "Christians are judgmental."[99] There's no sense in arguing with people's experiences by trying to defend Christians. The only way to help someone through this stage is to earn trust through friendship, which will take time and commitment. The pilgrim may test you to see if you're really interested in walking alongside them or just looking for a quick notch on your belt. For some, the damage will be too great to repair, and they may never get past this stage. The bad news is it only takes one Christian to cause someone to distrust all Christians. The good news is it only takes one Christian to help someone trust Christ. Be a patient, non-judgmental presence in someone's life, and let the Holy Spirit work. Christ converts; we don't.

Becoming Curious: "Jesus is interesting."

As we build friendships and form a community, we will be looking for a moment of spiritual curiosity in the pilgrim. In the Gospels, this moment often follows a miraculous

---

[99]. "A New Generation Expresses Its Skepticism and Frustration with Christianity," *Barna*, September 21, 2007, barna.com/research/a-new-generation-expresses-its-skepticism-and-frustration-with-christianity/.

encounter with the peculiar and hope-giving Christ. Jesus tells Peter to cast out his net and the nets are filled to the point of breaking. Jesus tells Nathanial he saw him under the fig tree. It's just crazy enough to pique their interest. In your fresh expression, you will build loving community so people can experience the miracle of belonging. But who knows what other miracles Jesus might have up his sleeve?

These moments of encounter with Christ in beloved community can happen anywhere. Barbara Holmes writes,

> We are told that Jesus hung out with publicans, tax collectors, and sinners. Perhaps during these sessions of music, laughter, and food fellowship, there were also sacred moments when the love of God and mutual care and concern became the focus of their time together. Contemplation is not confined to designated and institutional sacred spaces. God breaks into nightclubs and Billie Holiday's sultry torch songs; God tap dances with Bill Robinson and Savion Glover. And when Coltrane blew his horn, the angels paused to consider.[100]

An encounter with Christ leads to curiosity and the desire to know more about this guy named Jesus. This is a great time to invite the person into reading Gospel stories with you. The pilgrim will have lots of questions, and they'll likely find things they greatly admire about Jesus. We had an "atheist anarchist" come to King Street Church for a few months because he liked Jesus' politics. His ideological curiosity was an opportunity for us to introduce him to other aspects of Jesus' life and teaching.

---

100. Barbara A. Holmes, *Joy Unspeakable: Contemplative Practices of the Black Church*, 2nd ed. (Fortress: 2017), 183–184.

The wrong way to walk alongside someone in this stage is to answer all of their questions. Instead, get out of Jesus' way. In the Gospels, he stirs the pilgrim's imagination, he tells stories, he asks questions, he challenges their status quo, he confuses, he leaves room for wrestling, and only a few times he explains. Jesus is asked 183 questions in the Gospels and answers three directly.[101] In fact, Jesus responds to those 183 questions with 307 questions of his own! Don't quench a pilgrim's curiosity with over-simplified and uncompelling answers. Your answers might be wrong anyway. Savor the mystery with them, ask more questions, and save your brilliant insights for later.

We do no favors by introducing the Christian faith as something simple and easily understood. As Tomáš Halík notes, "When someone is introduced into the faith they need to be told clearly that they are being introduced into a world of mystery and depth."[102] We don't need to jump into the depths of theological discourse, but at the same time we must prepare the pilgrim for a journey that will be void of easy answers and frequently filled with doubts and divine silence. It is an exciting and joy-filled experience to walk with someone who is encountering Jesus with fresh eyes. Enjoy it and let their excitement rub off on you a bit.

Opening Up to Change: "Jesus could be for me."

This is the stage where personal reflection begins and an openness to change emerges. Not only will the pilgrim find Jesus interesting, but perhaps they will realize that his teaching has something to say to how they are living today. This threshold is often crossed when the pilgrim has a person, or better

---

101. Everts and Shaupp, *Pathway to Jesus,* 183.
102. Halík, *Night of the Confessor*, 58.

yet a community, showing them what Jesus' teachings look like in practice. As Elaine Heath puts it, "The proper context for evangelism is authentic Christian community, where the expression of loving community is the greatest apologetic for the gospel."[103] There is no greater testament to the love of God than to experience belonging in Christian community. When a pilgrim sees the radical love of Christ lived out in a community, they will compare it with their previous experiences in the world. There are not many other communities committed to unconditional acceptance, enemy love, and prioritizing the outcast and broken. When the pilgrim tastes the kingdom of God, a change of direction becomes tempting.

Seeking after God: "Jesus is worth taking seriously."

This is the stage when the pilgrim begins seeking a new way of life. Jesus offers a simple invitation: "Follow me." When we first accept this invitation, it is exploratory. The stage of exploration can move forward, but it can also come to a screeching halt. Plenty of those who followed Christ throughout Galilee drifted back to their old lives eventually—especially as Jerusalem loomed closer. At King Street Church we had several folks join us for a while and ultimately decide that following Jesus was not for them.

As a pilgrim seeks to follow Christ, you will begin to guide them in right habits and beliefs. This occurs in a mix of didactic learning (like school) and apprenticeship lived out in the fresh expression. In this stage, the approach to didactic learning should still be conversational, inviting folks into

---

103. Elaine A. Heath, *The Mystic Way of Evangelism: A Contemplative Vision for Christian Outreach* (Grand Rapids: Baker Academic, 2017), 13.

intentional conversations about Scripture and everyday life. Barbara Brown Taylor reflects,

> When people want to know more about God, the son of God tells them to pay attention to the lilies of the field and the birds of the air, to women kneading bread and workers lining up for their pay. Whoever wrote this stuff believed that people could learn as much about the ways of God from paying attention to the world as they could from paying attention to scripture.[104]

Your role in this stage is to help the pilgrim discover God all around them. At King Street Church, each of our gatherings began with a reading from Scripture. The leader would ask three to five open-ended questions about how the verse spoke to everyone's lives. When my friend J. R. Briggs asked Eugene Peterson what the role of the pastor in a congregation was, he responded, "To help people pay attention to God and respond appropriately."[105] What a perfect task for you as a guide in this stage of the sacred journey of discipleship.

Entering the Kingdom: "I'll turn to Jesus."

Mike Breen points out that discipleship is a careful dance between invitation and challenge. Jesus alternates between words of welcome, such as "my yoke is easy," and words of challenge, such as "get behind me, Satan." Much of the church overemphasizes challenge, trying to convince people of their sinfulness so they will begin a discipleship journey. The rest of the church seems to dismiss challenge all together.

---

104. Barbara Brown Taylor, *An Altar in the World: A Geography of Faith* (New York: HarperOne, 2010), 13.
105. J. R. Briggs, *Fail: Finding Hope and Grace in the Midst of Ministry Failure* (Downers Grove, IL: InterVaristy Press, 2014), 62.

In a fresh expression, building community is our act of invitation. We create a safe environment where hospitality and welcome can be felt. In exploring discipleship, we carefully begin to introduce acts of challenge. As a guide, you have been observing the pilgrim's actions and habits. Where have you seen areas in need of attention? With enough trust and tenderness, you can invite the pilgrim into another way of life. One man I met in the county jail likes to tell the story of when I asked him, "You've tried a lot of different ways of living. Why not try following Jesus?" He sees this moment as a major turning point in his life.

The mountaintop of the discipleship journey is repentance and belief in Jesus. In repentance, the pilgrim sees herself in a true light, recognizing that she has fallen short of who she was created to be. As she puts her faith in Christ and accepts the free gift of grace, the angels rejoice, for the lost is found. Be sure to celebrate these mountaintop moments as a fresh expression too!

I met James at our fresh expression of church in the county jail. James had been arrested a few months before on some serious drug charges and was awaiting his court date. Not long after arriving at the jail, he was given a Bible. Every week our group opened Scripture together, listening for God's voice to speak to us. A month later, James told us he had made a decision to give his life to Christ. He told us he wanted to be baptized but didn't know when it could happen. I replied, "How about next week?"

The next week we entered the pod (a common area in the jail connected to multiple cells) with a plastic pitcher of water and a stainless-steel basin. The automatic metal door locked behind us with a loud click. We sat down with James at the metal table and reviewed the basics of baptism. We stood up and a few other inmates came out of their cells.

James committed to the baptismal vows, which seemed to take on a deeper meaning in jail. The second vow says, "Do you accept the freedom and power God gives you to resist evil, injustice, and oppression in whatever forms they present themselves?"[106] In a place where he was stripped of most of his freedoms, James accepted a greater freedom that no bars could keep from him. James leaned over the metal basin, and I baptized him in the name of the Father, of the Son, and of the Holy Spirit. The water was dripping down his smiling face as I announced with pride, "Now it is our joy to welcome our new brother in Christ." The pod erupted with applause. The men standing out in the pod clapped, my co-leader clapped, and I even noticed one of the men still in bed in his cell popped his hands out of his blanket and clapped. The angels rejoiced, and James was beaming. We laid hands on him and prayed. One of the first things he said was, "I can't wait to tell my grandma." Just one story like that nearly makes it all worth it, doesn't it?

Living in the Kingdom: "Help me to live like Jesus."

Upon repentance and justification, the pilgrim begins a life-long process of growing in love of God and love of neighbor, becoming more dead to sin and more alive to God. This occurs as we form good habits and right beliefs. These habits include prayer, reading Scripture in solitude and in community, Communion, worship, fasting, acts of service, and acts of justice. The more we grow, the more others-centered we become, and the more we long for others to find freedom from oppression. James quickly discovered that following

---

106. "The Baptismal Covenant I," *UMC Discipleship*, 2009, umcdiscipleship.org/book-of-worship/the-baptismal-covenant-i.

Christ in the county jail was not easy. We watched him wrestle with his new way of life. He regularly shared about his challenges with non-violence. It was not easy to walk away from people who disrespected him; normally, he would settle disputes the old-fashioned way. He had to develop new habits and practices to handle conflicts.

Mike Breen points out that our habits and beliefs are formed by didactic learning, apprenticeship, and immersion. Didactic learning in a fresh expression is conversational and begins with discussing the basics of faith. Start with parables and stories about Jesus and slowly move into other areas of Scripture. Christ is revealed in the shared experiences and wisdom of those gathered around Scripture. Thomas Merton put it well when he said, "Since we are united as 'members one of another,' the living, salvific will of God is mysteriously communicated to us through one another."[107] I am often amazed at the insights people bring into these conversations and grateful that I didn't try to say it all myself.

Apprenticeship occurs as leaders of the fresh expression demonstrate following Christ to others in the group. I remember a surprisingly vulnerable moment when one of my excessively tattooed hardcore punk guys said to me, "I really admire the relationship you have with your wife. I hope I can have that someday." He had been watching how I lived, and it made him want to live that way too. Jesus leans heavily on the apprenticeship model in his ministry. He says in Matthew,

> Are you tired? Worn out? Burned out on religion? Come to me. Get away with me and you'll recover your life. I'll show you how to take a real rest. Walk with me and work with me—watch how I do it. Learn the unforced

---

107. Thomas Merton, *Life and Holiness* (New York: Image, 2014), 38.

> rhythms of grace. I won't lay anything heavy or ill-fitting on you. Keep company with me and you'll learn to live freely and lightly.[108]

Immersion is the learning that occurs in community life. I was educated as a social worker, and social workers will tell you that in group social work the interaction of the group transforms people far more than any content the leader introduces. Michael Moynagh calls this the "hidden curriculum."[109] In the context of community, our own sin is revealed. When folks at King Street Church committed to be in relationship with one another, it forced them to work on their brokenness. A woman recognized that the political rhetoric she had adopted from social media dehumanized another woman in the group. The conflict that arose helped her realize her own brokenness. In community we learn how to live with one another, how to forgive one another, and how to put others ahead of ourselves.

Another important element of living like Jesus is to join him in the work of making all things new. This work can be understood as ushering in *shalom,* or the perfection of God's creation. Lisa Sharon Harper writes,

> Shalom is what the Kingdom of God smells like. It's what the Kingdom looks like and what Jesus requires of the Kingdom's citizens. It's when everyone has enough. It's when families are healed. It's when shame is renounced and inner freedom is laid hold of. It's when human dignity, bestowed by the image of God in all humanity, is cultivated, protected and served in

---

108. Matthew 11:28–30 (MSG).
109. Michael Moynagh, *Being Church, Doing Life* (Oxford, England: Monarch Books, 2014), 182.

> families, faith communities, and schools and through public policy.[110]

Don't limit discipleship to the individual's relationship with God. Discipleship forms the individual as a member of the church and as a co-laborer with Christ in the redemption of all creation.

Inviting Others to Join: "My friends should know Jesus too."

As the pilgrim grows in their faith, they respond by inviting their friends into a discipleship journey of their own. Fresh Expressions can be an exponential growth movement in this way. In traditional forms of church, we ask people to come to us. Therefore, if a person joins our church, they start to spend more time with church people at the church building and less time with their friends and social connections in the community (who are likely unchurched). In a fresh expression, we form church in the places where people live and play. Therefore, it's easier for the pilgrim to maintain relationships with their unchurched friends and invite these friends into the fresh expression. In this way the journey of discipleship never ends and never stops replicating.

A Real-Life Discipleship Journey

When Erica started coming to King Street Church, she identified as "spiritual but not religious." Early on she told me that she prayed to a god, but she was not sure who this god was. You might say she was praying to an *unknown god* (Acts 17). She described mystical encounters in prayer that she had

---

110. Lisa Sharon Harper, *The Very Good Gospel: How Everything Wrong Can Be Made Right* (Colorado Springs: Waterbrook, 2018), 14.

experienced, something I recognized as the Holy Spirit actively speaking to her. After a year of participating in weekly discussions about Scripture, she told me that she now realized the God we were reading about was the God she had been praying to, but she didn't understand why she needed Jesus as anything other than a wise teacher. I told her not to worry too much about it, and just to keep coming. Another year later, in her personal reading of the passion story in John, she had a mystical encounter with Jesus, feeling his shame on the cross in a deep and unexplainable way. She told me she now understood why she needed Jesus. I told her she was a Christian now. She replied, "No way!" Her journey to faith in Christ took over two years.

Knowing how gradual conversion can be, it's easy to see how inviting non-Christians to Sunday morning worship is largely ineffective at bringing people into the faith. It is too big a jump for most. In our post-Christian age, people need time to test the waters, to pursue faith at their own pace without pressure to conform. Not only do we need forms of church willing to go to where our post-Christian friends spend their time, we need forms of church willing to travel this slow pace alongside them. Fresh expressions are designed to be this kind of community.

Further Reading:

Mike Breen, *Building a Discipling Culture: How to Release a Missional Movement by Discipling People like Jesus Did* (Greenville, SC: 3DM Publishing, 2017).

Breen's work, along with that of Bob and Mary Hopkins and others, in Sheffield, UK, was highly influential in the beginnings of the Fresh Expressions movement, and his writing on discipleship has been equally influential. This book is an excellent companion for this stage of the journey.

Russell Brand, *Mentors: How to Help and Be Helped* (New York: Henry Holt, 2019).

Brand is known for being an outrageous comedian, but if you read any of his books or listen to his interviews, you will see he is quite brilliant. In this book, he uses his experiences in Alcoholics Anonymous and other areas of his fascinating life to introduce some important reflections on mentorship. (Fair warning: unsurprisingly it's a PG-13 read.)

Accompanying Prayer
A Collect for Exploring Discipleship

O Christ, your invitation and challenge to each person is always shaped by careful attention to where they are on the journey. Give us that sensitivity—attune us to the pace of each pilgrim, and alert us to when and how we can help them cross thresholds. Make our communities like rich soil for each disciple's development—immerse us in practices of wisdom and wonder which draw us into the love of the Father, who reigns with you and the Holy Spirit, one God, further up and further in. *Amen.*

— Terry Stokes

Chapter Six

CHURCH TAKING SHAPE

"Word and sacrament and the journey into holiness. These will survive, whatever happens to this or that style of worship, this or that bit of Christian culture, because the presence of Jesus in the community will survive."
— Rowan Williams

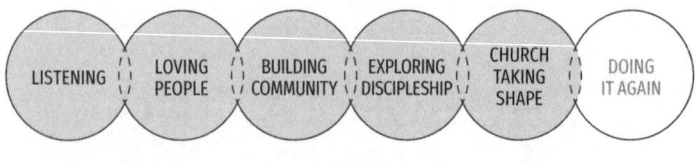

UNDERPINNED BY PRAYER AND CONTINUING CONNECTION TO THE WIDER CHURCH

The route of the Appalachian Trail (AT) has changed constantly over the past eighty years. These changes occur for a myriad of reasons, including erosion, the construction of dams that redirect rivers, and changes in the understanding of trail construction (we zigzag up mountains now; back in the day they hiked straight up). Old paths often return to nature when new routes are created. Jim Neely, a retired prosecutor with entirely too much time on his hands, has spent years carefully researching this "Lost Appalachian Trail." Specifically, he has studied a section of around 300 miles in Virginia that was abandoned and relocated in the 1950s following hurricane damage and the construction of the Blue Ridge Parkway.[111] Neely has fond memories of hiking the "new trail" in 1962 and remembers hearing about this old trail, so he carefully reconstructed the 1950 map and did his best to hike it. He hopes his work will "give recognition to the quality of that Old AT route and to the many dedicated

---

111. Laurence Hammack, "Did the Man Heralded as the First to Walk the Entire Appalachian Trail Take a Shortcut into History?" *The Roanoke Times*, July 2, 2011, roanoke.com/webmin/news/did-the-man-heralded-as-the-first-to-walk-the/article_08e4e205-f2f3-57ee-8528-d81c148bfb2a.html.

individuals who labored to bring that Trail into existence and maintained it for nearly a quarter-century."[112]

As folks in your fresh expression move forward in their discipleship journey, some will be ready for more elements of church. Some will desire a more intentional worship service, others might want to pray together, others might be interested in the sacraments. This is a natural move from biblical basics to sacramental depths. As these elements are added to the fresh expression, a church begins to take shape. The problem is, most of us carry a vision of church that is based more in what we are used to than what is needed for new disciples. We need to spend time working on our ecclesiology—our understanding of the nature and structure of church. Our present ecclesiology is like trying to navigate the Appalachian Trail in 2020 with a map of the trail from 1950.[113] Our dated ideas about the structure of church end up working against us. As Tony Campolo says, "If the 1950s ever comes back, the church will be ready."[114] It's time to reconsider what makes something a church.

What Is Church?

As King Street Church was beginning to take shape, I was haunted by the question, "Is this church?" Everything about it felt like church—the fellowship, the centrality of Scripture

---

112. Jim McNeely, "The Old Appalachian Trail in the New River Valley 1931–1955," *New River Symposium* (May 2017), vtechworks.lib.vt.edu/bitstream/handle/10919/89782/NRSPresentation516.pdf?sequence=1&isAllowed=y.
113. Alan Hirsch put it this way: "Our ecclesiology is like trying to navigate New York City with a map of London." Alan Hirsch, presentation at Fresh Expressions US National Gathering, Reston Virginia, March 15, 2018.
114. Brian D. McLaren and Anthony Campolo, *Adventures in Missing the Point: How the Culture-Controlled Church Neutered the Gospel* (Grand Rapids: Zondervan, 2006), 158.

to our gatherings, the sharing of meals—but it sure didn't look like any churches around, especially ones in my denomination. Our understanding of church impacts how we form church as a fresh expression. The problem is, not many of us have spent much time reflecting on the simple question, "What is church?"

So what makes something church? In *An Introduction to Ecclesiology*, Veli-Matti Kärkkäinen offers a fascinating look into how various traditions have defined church. You might expect debates on how many presbyters to have, how often to have committee meetings, who will be on which rota, or whether bishops get to wear the cool hats or not. But no, theologians across traditions seeking to define church seem far less concerned with patterns and practices and far more concerned with the presence of the Trinitarian God.[115] And where is the presence of God?

Jesus tells us that he is present *where two or three gather in my name* (Matt. 18:20). Diane Anderson, a lay person at United Presbyterian Church in Paterson, New Jersey, said it well: "Church is wherever people are gathered in the name of God. And wherever the Word of God is, is where the sanctuary is. So for us the sanctuary could be on the corner of the street, it could be in the laundromat, it's wherever there are people."[116] With this definition of church, she has started a worshiping community called Faith Works among those struggling with addiction and those working in prostitution in her neighborhood. When we gather around Jesus together, we are the church.

---

115. Veli-Matti Kärkkäinen, *An Introduction to Ecclesiology: Ecumenical, Historical & Global Perspectives* (Downers Grove, IL: InterVarsity Press, 2002).
116. 1001 New Worshipping Communities, "Faith Works: Wings and a Prayer," YouTube video, 2:16, August 21, 2015, youtube.com/watch?v=mV_pzcuV5KE.

Chapter Six | Church Taking Shape

What Do We Need to Have Church?

At dinner the other night, I asked my mother-in-law to describe how she packed for a weeklong journey on the trail. She replied, "I take only what I need. Every ounce matters." If her backpack weighs too much, it will result in an injury and keep her from finishing her journey. She tries to get her pack to weigh less than seventeen pounds before adding food and water to minimize the impact on her back and knees. This is not an easy feat between a backpack, tent, sleeping bag, sleeping pad, water filter, stove, and fuel, but over the years she has figured out ways to trim off ounces. She cut off the unnecessary straps on her backpack, bought lighter equipment, and even sawed off half the handle of her toothbrush. Thru-hikers find creative ways to carry the least amount of equipment while maintaining the minimum amount of supplies they need for their journey. The church must start thinking this way. What would it look like for us to trim church down without losing what's essential? What is the extra weight of ministry that is holding us back on our journey?

Simon Bonnington is a physician in Nova Scotia. When the circuit pastor of his small Canadian Baptist congregation in Port Lorne died suddenly, the church faced a dilemma: how to replace a pastor without enough money coming in. So the group decided to look at what the Bible says about being church. In reading Scripture together, they rediscovered the power of the priesthood of all believers (1 Peter 2:9). After much conversation, they decided not to replace their pastor and chose instead to "do church themselves." Simon says of the congregation today, "We are a group of people in their sixties and seventies, discovering what it is to be personally faithful within worship." These days, they each take turns leading prayer, Scripture reading, short homilies, and hymn singing. Without a pastor stipend, the group is able to support the local foodbank and the Salvation Army poverty-relief program. Bonnington added, "They've discovered churching is a fun thing to do!" When you start a fresh expression, you have the chance to create a church in its simplest form. So ask yourself, what do you need? What can you do without and still have church?

Form Follows Mission

The hope of the fresh expressions journey is not to make disciples to fill the Sunday morning pews, but to create a church for those disconnected from church as we know it. Therefore, as you see disciples growing in your fresh expression, you will begin to recognize that those who started with milk are ready for some meat. The temptation will be to create a worship service that's just slightly edgier than your contemporary service on Sunday morning. Instead, in fresh expressions we reflect upon the basic elements of church, paying particular attention to our tradition, and we seek to add these elements to our fresh expression in new and creative ways. Church structure takes shape as we reflect on which elements of church the members of our fresh expression are ready to explore.

Sara Williams and Dan Carlson reflect on how this process played out at Noon Service, an Episcopal fresh expression in Cincinnati:

> Again and again, we heard people describe church as a place where one goes to watch or have something done for you. What they desired was a place to dialogue and act with others. From these insights, the Noon Service was born. . . . We kept the liturgy simple, we made community conversation a central part of the "homiletic

event," and we invited musicians to create music that connected ancient words with modern melodies.[117]

Architect Louis Sullivan wrote in 1896, "Whether it be the sweeping eagle in his flight, or the open apple-blossom, the toiling work-horse, the blithe swan, the branching oak, the winding stream at its base, the drifting clouds, over all the coursing sun, form ever follows function, and this is the law."[118] In a fresh expression, we might phrase it a little differently: *form follows mission*. When your fresh expression begins meeting, the form of the gathering is shaped by the need to create a community of welcoming and belonging. As discipleship begins to take place, the gathering shifts or a new gathering begins, and the form is shaped by the need to create meaningful dialogue and spiritual growth. Now we must think through what form of gathering will help the group become a church—that is, the living body of Christ.

An unfortunate side effect of our historical deficiency in the American Church is we think our forms of church have always been the same. The Anglican Articles of Religion dating back to the sixteenth century, however, show us otherwise: "It is not necessary that Traditions and Ceremonies be in all places one, or utterly like; for at all times they have been diverse, and may be changed according to the diversity

---

117. Sara Williams, Dan Carlson, and Jane Gerdsen, "Giving Away the Church: Reflections on Fresh Ecclesial Expressions," *Earth and Altar*, accessed May 13, 2020, earthandaltarmag.com/posts/giving-way-the-church-reflections-on-fresh-ecclesial-expressions.
118. Louis H. Sullivan, "The Tall Office Building Artistically Considered," *Lippincott's*, 1896, ocw.mit.edu/courses/architecture/4-205-analysis-of-contemporary-architecture-fall-2009/readings/MIT4_205F09_Sullivan.pdf.

of countries, times, and men's manners, so that nothing be ordained against God's Word."[119]

The forms and structures of the church have always been changing. And they continue to change in our time, adapting to our current needs and values.[120]

Thinking About Context

It's vital to form a church that is culturally appropriate for the population in which it emerges. We have to resist the impulse to simply import the form of church we are most familiar with. This is the work of contextualization. Richard Twiss writes, "Contextualization is a relational process of theological and cultural reflection within a community—seeking to incorporate traditional symbols, music, dance, ceremony and ritual to make faith in Jesus a truly local expression."[121]

As Twiss emphasizes throughout his book, *Rescuing the Gospel from the Cowboys*, such contextualization should emerge from the local population—an outsider cannot do the work of contextualization without leaning on local leadership. Boone, North Carolina, is a town known for its laid-back mountain lifestyle. So when a megachurch from "down the mountain" tried to start a remote campus in town, it didn't go so well. Instead of adapting to this new context, they carbon-copied the big city campus model, projecting a video of their trendy pastor and following it with a highly produced worship service that fell flat. People move to Boone to get away from the big city, so no amount of marketing or iPad

---

119. "Articles of Religion," *Anglicans Online*, updated May 23, 2017, anglicansonline.org/basics/thirty-nine_articles.html.
120. Priya Parker, "You Can't Put the Baby Back In," *Together Apart*, audio, 10:45, podcasts.apple.com/us/podcast/together-apart/id1506057555?i=1000472225167.
121. Richard Twiss, *Rescuing the Gospel from the Cowboys: A Native American Expression of the Jesus Way* (Downers Grove, IL: InterVarsity, 2015), 15.

giveaways could've saved this venture. They failed to contextualize their church to our community, and it didn't last long.

Note that you can take contextualization too far. Marva Dawn warns, "Worship that is too much like the world can hardly redescribe it."[122] A faithful gathering of the church will always be at odds with the world around it because the gospel is an invitation into a new life and a new vision of community.

Marks of the Church, Reimagined

What you might call the first Christian worship gathering occurred on a trail. Cleopas and another disciple were walking from Jerusalem to a village called Emmaus, processing the news they had just heard, that Jesus was alive. As they walked, Jesus joined them, but somehow they didn't recognize him. As the three of them walked, Jesus explained the Scriptures from Exodus to the Prophets regarding the Messiah. What I would give to hear this sermon! When they reached Emmaus, the disciples invited their new friend in for dinner. And in the breaking of bread, Jesus was revealed to them and then disappeared. They said to one another, "Were not our hearts burning within us while he talked with us on the road and opened the Scriptures to us?"[123] They left at once to proclaim the Good News of the resurrected Christ to the others. In this dramatic episode from the Gospel of Luke, we witness the basic elements of church come together for the first time: Word, sacrament, worship, fellowship, and mission.[124] For the last 2,000 years, the church has never stopped adapting these

---

122. Marva J. Dawn, *A Royal Waste of Time: The Splendor of Worshiping God and Being Church for the World* (Grand Rapids: Eerdmans, 1999), 339. (Via Moynagh, *Church for Every Context*, 362.)
123. Luke 24:32.
124. "The Basic Pattern of Worship," *UMC Discipleship*, 1992, umcdiscipleship.org/book-of-worship/the-basic-pattern-of-worship.

elements. How will you incorporate these elements into your fresh expression of church?

Proclamation of the Word. The very center of the church's calling is the proclamation of the Word. Church history shows that the form of proclamation has gone through dramatic changes over time. There are other ways to proclaim the Word of God than lectures (a product of the Enlightenment). Forms like conversational preaching can capture and keep the attention of those exploring and growing in the Christian faith. Lucy Atkinson Rose writes, "In conversational preaching, the preacher and the congregation are colleagues, exploring together the mystery of the word for their own lives, as well as the life of the congregation, the larger church, and the world."[125]

At King Street Church, I prepared and led weekly discussions around passages of Scripture. I prepared these discussions similarly to preparing a sermon. However, my goal was to draw proclamation from the people around the table, chiming in with my thoughts only when necessary. I was constantly amazed at the group's ability to proclaim the meaning and promises of God's Word together, even the folks who were not Christians. There were insights others around the table provided that I never could. Christ is revealed in the shared experiences and wisdom of those gathered around Scripture. Instead of preparing a moving speech, I spent time crafting questions that would help our people to proclaim the Good News gleaned from their own insights and experiences.

Sacraments. This book is for a wide variety of Christian traditions, so writing about the sacraments feels like charging into a minefield. Your tradition's sacramental theology may

---

125. Lucy Atkinson Rose, *Sharing the Word: Preaching in the Roundtable Church* (Louisville: Westminster John Knox, 2000), 4.

Chapter Six | Church Taking Shape

be very different than mine. Be sure to consult with your senior pastor or denominational supervisor before incorporating the sacraments into your fresh expression. Many traditions will require a clergyperson to lead the sacraments. For lay-led fresh expressions, this might mean inviting in the pastor of your anchor church for Communion. In most of these traditions, you as a lay leader will be able to assist in administering the sacraments.

In my tradition, United Methodism, we celebrate two sacraments: baptism and Communion. In the mystery of baptism, we are spiritually born anew and initiated into the community of the church. I will never forget baptizing an infant at our fresh expression in the homeless shelter. A group of residents gathered in the courtyard of the shelter to support the child and her parents. The moment I finished the baptismal liturgy, a downpour of rain fell, reminding us all of our baptisms as we scurried inside. In the mystery of Communion, we receive grace and experience sanctification, thanksgiving, remembrance, and fellowship. Leading Communion in the county jail was a particularly powerful experience. On the other hand, members of King Street Church often carried great emotional baggage from previous experiences at the Lord's Table. One night at KSC, the week after a major conflict, I decided to serve Communion in the hopes of bringing our community together. What I did not foresee was that half of those in attendance refused the sacrament due to feelings of doubt or unworthiness. The Eucharist exacerbated the division in the group. Fortunately, I was able to respond with a conversation about the unwarranted grace of God and the invitation to Christ's table that is extended to all. The sacraments are gifts, but they've been fought over and left folks scarred. Surprisingly, they can also be a source of healing, even *the* source of healing, in your fresh expression.

Worship. When I tell people about King Street Church, I am often asked, "Where is the worship?" What they mean is, "Where is the music?" The church of the last forty years, much to our detriment, has fused the language of worship and music. Equating worship to singing three guitar songs with three guitar chords creates a limited understanding of the rich vision of Christian worship and stifles our missional potential. It takes a long time for a convert to be able to sing the words of devotion and sacrifice found in our hymns and worship songs. Imagine singing a love song on your first date. That's awkward.

Worship is a transformative encounter with God—no melody required. Every moment of a church gathering, from prayer, to the reading of God's word, to proclamation, to participating in Holy Communion, is worship. Music certainly has a great potential to be a way to worship, but so is communal reading, sharing a testimony, or prayer.

According to the renowned biblical scholar N. T. Wright, "Christian worship . . . is all about telling the story of what God has done, is doing, and will do. . . . It celebrates God's mighty deeds, and, by the sheer fact of doing so, helps forward the next stage of God's purpose."[126] "Jesus, Jazz & Dessert Wine@Vespers" (JJDW) is an online faith community hosted by Alexus Rhone. They gather around storytelling and jazz. Alexus, known as Lex, says that adults need story time just as much as children, and in this digital gathering, they explore "the intersection of art, faith, and the ongoing battle for a language that defines reality."[127] JJDW's gatherings

---

126. N. T. Wright, "Freedom and Framework, Spirit and Truth: Recovering Biblical Worship," *N. T. Wright*, April 5, 2016, ntwrightpage.com/2016/04/05/freedom-and-framework-spirit-and-truth-recovering-biblical-worship-2/.

127. Alexus Rhone, "Jesus, Jazz & Dessert Wine@Vespers, featuring Tina Morris Robertson," YouTube video, 46:49, November 21, 2020, youtu.be/wIwpff4vcNA.

include a time of jazz with Lynette Barber, storytelling by Lex (and special guests), lament, and prophetic hope. They close with a blessing and sending. You can find their next gathering at alexusrhone.com. In a fresh expression, the first step is to incorporate missional worship—a taste of worship for seekers.[128] As the fresh expression matures, you can gradually shift into fuller forms of worship.

Edification of Believers. An essential aspect of church is the supporting and equipping of its members. This includes discipleship as well as pastoral care for those in your fresh expression. The journey of discipleship described in the last chapter doesn't end at conversion. We will spend the rest of our lives learning how to follow Jesus more closely, and we need companions as the journey continues. That might mean reading a book together, bringing in mentors from your anchor church, or hosting a women's group. It's important to retain small groups where discipleship can occur as your fresh expression grows and changes.

Pastoral care looks very different in a fresh expression. I would often meet members of King Street Church for a cup of coffee or a beer at the pub when they were facing a difficult situation or decision. Share the load of pastoral care with others in the group who are gifted in this area, and remember, it's almost never about giving the best advice; often, it's about being the best listener. Be sure to conclude a meeting like this with a prayer for the person. If you feel unable to offer appropriate care for someone, don't hesitate to reach out to your pastor or connect someone to a local counselor. If someone is requesting pastoral care on a regular basis, that's a good sign they need a professional counselor.

---

128. Michael Moynagh, *Being Church, Doing Life* (Oxford, England: Monarch Books, 2014), 189.

Justice and Mission. Earlier in the book, I warned against building a community based on one-way service. However, as your fresh expression has taken shape, you have built relationships with people in the community, and community members have taken leadership roles in your fresh expression, and now your group is ready to identify an injustice that it wishes to address. This should emerge from the group as a response to careful listening to the community. At King Street Church, half of our congregation had a rap sheet. Our people had experienced firsthand the near impossible barriers facing folks as they leave incarceration and enter back into wider society. Therefore, reentry became an issue we could unite behind and work to address. We saw men and women stuck in a vicious cycle of incarceration and homelessness who desperately needed mental health care or addiction treatment. Yet our state and federal government increased funding for prison-building and decreased funding for mental health and addiction. So our church advocated for reforms and saw a change of culture occur in the community. In 2019, a diversion program took effect in Watauga County, redirecting people accused of low-level crimes away from pointless incarceration and toward the resources they needed.

Lilla Watson, an Aboriginal activist in Australia, gives an important warning, "If you have come here to help me, you are wasting your time. But if you have come because your liberation is bound up with mine, then let us work together."[129] Liberation is woven into love and belonging. So as you look for ways your fresh expression can help in your community, look for ways to walk alongside others, rather than handing down help from above.

---

129. Michael F. Leonen, "Etiquette for Activists," *Yes!*, May 21, 2004, yesmagazine.org/issue/hope-conspiracy/2004/05/21/etiquette-for-activists/.

Prayer. William Barry, the great Jesuit spiritual director, offers a helpful definition of prayer: "Prayer is a conscious, personal relationship with God."[130] To be conscious of God is to be aware of God's presence and to respond to that presence. In a fresh expression, prayer will take on various forms. Many fresh expressions open or close with a time of prayer. You will often find that people new to the faith are open to sharing prayer requests long before they are comfortable praying themselves. Keeping our definition in mind though, you might also find that people new to the faith have been praying long before they knew what to call it. Many of our folks at King Street Church who were new to Christianity had been aware of God's presence—while hiking in the outdoors, chanting for justice at protests, or writing poetry—they just needed a word to describe those experiences. Think about your context and where each individual is on their journey and help move them forward in their prayer life. I have found ancient prayers like the psalms and the examen, a prayerful reflection upon the previous day, to be a great way to help folks new to prayer get started.[131] If you need a way to introduce prayer to your community, check out @prayersfromterry on Instagram (he wrote the collects for this book). He writes traditional prayers for our contemporary world (some are fun, some quite serious). My favorite is a prayer "For when one walks out the door looking fly."[132]

Giving. The closest I've been to getting punched in church was at a Fresh Expressions training where I said that fresh

---

130. William A. Barry, *God and You: Prayer as a Personal Relationship* (New York: Paulist Press, 1987), 76.
131. See "Reimagining the Examen App," *Ignatian Spirituality*, accessed May 28, 2020, ignatianspirituality.com/reimagining-examen-app/.
132. Terry Stokes (@prayersfromterry), *Instagram*, accessed June 28, 2020, instagram.com/prayersfromterry/.

expressions often don't include an offering. After the session, a woman, visibly shaking, told me you can't have church without an offering. It was clear she had the gift of generosity and put a high value on this element of church as a result. What I tried to explain was that in fresh expressions we meet people where they are and help them move forward from there. The reality is that most of the people you connect with will not be ready to tithe to a church for a long time—there is too much distrust in the church regarding money and giving. It's not worth the risk of scaring someone off by introducing an offering too soon. Church lady Evander Holyfield obviously disagreed.

If we reflect on the meaning behind tithing, we find that it's about recognizing that all we have is a gift from God, responding to the invitation of Christ to live a generous life, and giving back to God a portion of what we have been given. One way we did this at King Street Church was through inviting generosity for those on the margins. Every year we raised money to replenish our community "reentry fund," a fund housed at a local non-profit that helped folks in our community get a fresh start after incarceration. Church members donated their money to the fund and also had an opportunity to participate in planning and implementing our fundraisers. For three years we hosted a benefit concert called "Cash for Convicts," where area bands played Johnny Cash and Merle Haggard cover songs at the Boone Saloon. Each year it raised about $1,500 dollars. The last year I was at King Street Church, we partnered with a local coffee shop to roast our own coffee blend, The Second Chance Blend. Our King Streeters volunteered to sell coffee at area holiday markets and outside the local bakery. You'd be amazed at how many bags of coffee a former drug dealer can sell on a Saturday morning.

So how do fresh expressions become financially sustainable without tithes? Most fresh expressions have to keep their budgets low and rely on donors. At King Street Church our biggest expense was me. In the early years, I supplemented part-time ministry with side hustles; my favorite was being a fly fishing guide for a local resort. Later on, denominational grants and our anchor church generously supported more of my salary. A large percentage of fresh expressions are layled and have no paid staff, or the fresh expression is just one aspect of a paid staff person's responsibilities at the anchor church. As far as donors go, think about who resonates with your vision and mission. Our biggest donor at King Street Church, besides the United Methodist Church, was a local bail bondsman, who saw how we were making an impact on his clientele. As a faithful Christian, he was happy to see his repeat customers not need him anymore.

Resistance to Change. What church could be complete without the "Back to Egypt Committee"—that group of people who love to say, "We like the way things were!"[133] I include this as a mark of the church playfully, but also to prepare you for the inevitable. No matter how fresh your fresh expression is, your group will begin to become insular and some members will become protective of the status quo. I will never forget asking our group in the pub how we should adapt to an influx of new people. One heavily tattooed, church-averse young woman replied, "I don't want us to change. Why can't we stay the same?" Phrases I thought were limited to grumpy lifelong church members are actually a universal language. Look for the feelings beneath resistance to change—mainly the fear of losing something you love—and spend time

---

133. Greg Jones, "God's Great Generosity, *North Carolina Conference UMC*, June 17, 2017, nccumc.org/ac2017/2017/06/17/greg-jones-gods-great-generosity/.

unpacking these with your people. You can celebrate the season that is coming to a close and reassure your people that change is normal and necessary.

Change the Group or Start Another Gathering?

When transitioning your fresh expression from the exploring discipleship stage to the church taking shape stage we face a dilemma: change the discipleship group or start another gathering? The early church, expelled from their synagogues, gathered in homes for a two-part service, the service of the word and the service of table. The former was open to everyone—believers and seekers alike. The latter was only open to baptized Christians.[134] There is value in having distinct gatherings for distinct stages of faith.

N. T. Wright also notes, "Ideally every Christian should belong to a group that is small enough for individuals to get to know and care for each other, and particularly to pray in meaningful depth for one another, and also to a fellowship large enough to contain a wide variety in its membership, styles of worship, and kingdom-activity. The smaller the local community, the more important it is to be powerfully linked to a larger unit. . . . Ideally, groups of a dozen or so will meet to pray, study scripture, and build one another up in faith."[135]

You might be wondering, *How on earth are we going to manage all of these gatherings?* Know that not every gathering must be weekly. You might leave your weekly discipleship gathering untouched, but add a monthly gathering that reflects a more complete order of worship. Also know this is why a fresh expressions team is essential. You as a leader

---

134. Justo L. González, *The Story of Christianity Vol. 1: The Early Church to the Dawn of the Reformation* (New York: HarperOne, 2010), 35.
135. N. T. Wright, *Simply Christian* (New York: HarperOne, 2010), 212.

cannot be in charge of every gathering. You need a team you can rely on. Talk to your team and your regulars about these types of decisions.

The River of Life

Just outside Bryson City, North Carolina, Highway 19 follows the Nantahala River. As you meander down the gorge, mountains surround you on both sides until you reach the Nantahala Outdoor Center. The Nantahala Outdoor Center is a remarkable place, a village fully dedicated to "paddlers," a term that includes kayakers, rafters, and canoers. You can hire a guide, buy some gear, eat a gourmet lunch, or just jump in and paddle. It is here that Wayne Dickert, or Wayner as he is known by the paddling community, leads a fresh expression called River of Life. The fresh expression is anchored to Bryson City United Methodist where Wayner is also the pastor. River of Life is much farther along in the life cycle of a fresh expression than most in our conference: it has matured into a church that worships weekly.

As chairs are pulled together in the outdoor pub area overlooking the river, the group gathers in song. Then the offering is introduced. When I'm asked how fresh expressions take up an offering, I always refer to the River of Life. Instead of asking folks who attend to give to a salary or a church building, all giving goes to drilling wells in Haiti. It's a simple way to encourage generosity while not turning off those who mistrust the church. Next the service shifts toward an interactive message. Wayner's messages fit perfectly with the surroundings as well as the community he is speaking to, drawing from his experience as a guide and paddling instructor. After the message, Wayner introduces the response, a five-minute time of quiet individual reflection by the river. Attendees often cite this as their favorite part of worship. When the five minutes are up, a church leader collects everyone back for the benediction. After fifteen years, the river of life is still living into their vision of being the church with paddlers who otherwise wouldn't be connected to a church.

Becoming a Mature Expression of Church

When all of the essential elements of church are being incorporated regularly, the fresh expression of church becomes a mature expression of church. So how will you know when you have arrived? The Nicene-Constantinopolitan Creed, adopted by the church in 381 CE, offers us a helpful checklist. It reads, "We believe in the one holy catholic and apostolic church."

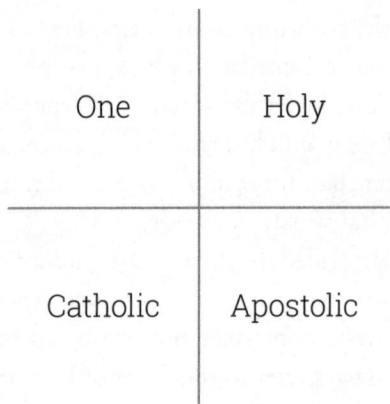

One. The church is the community and fellowship of believers. As I mentioned in an earlier chapter, we are one with one another, and one with God, joined with Christ. I have seen this in high steeple sanctuaries when a child runs up to their favorite elderly friend for a hug, and I have witnessed this in the "C Pod" of the Watauga County Jail where the inmates prayed for one another, studied Scripture together, and shared their meals together, all on a daily basis.

Holy. The Holy Spirit dwells in all the world, but in a concentrated way, beyond our understanding, in the church. The church is set apart and committed to discipleship and worship. The church is connected to the presence of the Trinitarian God through worship, proclamation of the Word, and participation in the sacraments. I've witnessed this in ancient churches following ancient liturgies and in conversations around a few tables pulled together in a pub.

Catholic. The church is universal. All who are baptized in the name of the Father, the Son, and Holy Spirit are members of the catholic (universal) church.[136] While maintaining our traditions and distinctives is important, all Christian churches throughout the world and throughout history are linked together as the Universal Church. The blended ecology of fresh expressions connected to anchor churches offers a beautiful image of this connection. Each one needs the other.

Apostolic. The church is consumed by an insatiable love and concern for the world around it. The church follows Christ in mission, witness, and service to the far reaches of the world. I've seen this in missionary believers scattered throughout the globe and in folks who check in on their elderly neighbors after a long day at work in rural Appalachia.[137]

---

136. *The Book of Common Prayer,* 876.
137. Luke Edwards, "What Is Church Anyways?" *Fresh Expressions US*, May 31, 2017, freshexpressionsus.org/2017/05/31/what-is-church-anyways/.

If you can check all four boxes, you might have a mature expression of church! Becoming a mature expression of church doesn't mean it will cease to be fresh or begin to look like a traditional form of church. It will likely still appear shockingly different to those accustomed to a certain way of being church. But don't let anyone convince you that your church is less-than or church-lite. Celebrate—you have reached the climax of your journey. It might have taken years, but you have arrived!

Further Reading:

Tim Lomax, *Creating Missional Worship: Fusing Context and Tradition* (London: Church House, 2015).

There's a tendency in fresh expressions to mimic contemporary worship or avoid worship altogether. Lomax offers rich insights into how to find a balance between carrying on our rich traditions and adapting to new contexts, particularly among the unchurched. He includes a ton of examples as well as some sample orders of worship.

Priya Parker, *The Art of Gathering: How We Meet and Why It Matters* (New York: Riverhead, 2018).

Parker is one of the leading voices in designing meaningful gatherings. In this book, she will push you to nail down your *why* first, and only then to think about *how* you will gather. Most of us (particularly in the church) get this backwards, repeating patterns of gathering with little thought as to how effective they might be.

Accompanying Prayer
A Collect for Church Taking Shape

O God, worshiped in as many unique ways as there are unique bodies of believers, establish in us forms of Word and sacrament that both reflect and create the new life we are pursuing together. Suspend our presuppositions—let our imagination of what church can look like be aided, not restricted, by what we've seen, as you did for the apostles. Shape us according to the oneness, wholeness, and holiness of the universal church, under the Lordship of Christ, who reigns with you and the Holy Spirit, one God, in glorious fellowship. *Amen.*

— Terry Stokes

Chapter Seven

DOING IT AGAIN

"We do not need a leader to get us out of this mess; we need a thousand leaders."
— Alexia Salvatierra

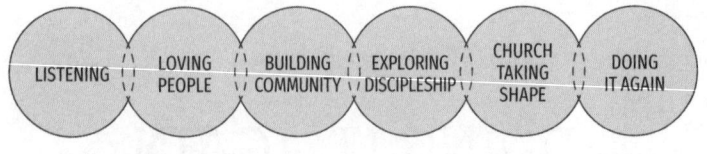

UNDERPINNED BY PRAYER AND CONTINUING CONNECTION TO THE WIDER CHURCH

In 2015, Elsye Walker, trail name "Chardonnay," completed the 2,000-mile Pacific Crest Trail. Soon after, she told one interviewer, "It is fair to say that I have been bitten by the thru-hiking bug!"[138] Three years later, she became the first African American woman to complete the "Triple Crown of Thru-Hiking," which includes the Appalachian Trail, the Pacific Crest Trail, and the Continental Divide Trail, altogether a whopping 8,000 miles. Reflecting on her accomplishment, she says,

> People are surprised to see a female, black thru-hiker. . . . At an outfitter recently, a guy asked if I was thinking about doing a thru-hike. When I told him I had done all three trails, he said, "Oh, I never imagined." It didn't matter if he imagined it; I imagined, believed, and did it. It's not about what people expect or think a thru-hiker looks like. It's about what is true.[139]

---

138. Teresa Baker, "It's All About the Journey. Hiking the PCT, solo.," *African American Explorations*, October 9, 2015, tmbaker1165.wordpress.com/2015/10/09/its-all-about-the-journey-hiking-the-pct-solo/.

139. Becky Booroojian, "Q&A with Elsye "Chardonnay" Walker: Likely the First Black, Female Triple Crowner," *The Trek*, September 10, 2018, thetrek.co/qa-elsye-chardonnay-walker-likely-first-black-female-triple-crowner/.

Reading through her hiking journals, you see that completing the first hike didn't necessarily make the following journeys any easier; each trail held its own unique challenges. And yet she persevered. When asked what was next for her, she replied, "I hear the Arizona Trail is nice in the fall . . . just sayin'."[140]

After experiencing the process of birthing a fresh expression, every member has the ability to start another one. Therefore, it's important that the first fresh expression is simple enough that members see they have the ability to start their own. Soon, individual fresh expressions can become networks of fresh expressions, and then a movement begins. In addition, denominational bodies can create Fresh Expressions movements within their regions. I've been a part of every level of the Fresh Expressions movement in the United States, and I have found three aspects of movement-building are important at every level: identifying potential leaders, training new leaders, and supporting existing leaders.

The Four Spaces of Belonging

Your fresh expression is growing. Now what? In previous chapters we've discussed the importance of shaping your gathering based on your purpose and present needs. The size of your fresh expression impacts the social interactions within it. The four spaces of belonging, created by Joseph Myers, is helpful for us in picturing what a network of fresh expressions might look like.[141]

---

140. Ibid.
141. For overview see JR Woodward and Dan White, *The Church as Movement: Starting and Sustaining Missional-Incarnational Communities* (Downers Grove, IL: InterVarsity Press, 2016), 155–160.

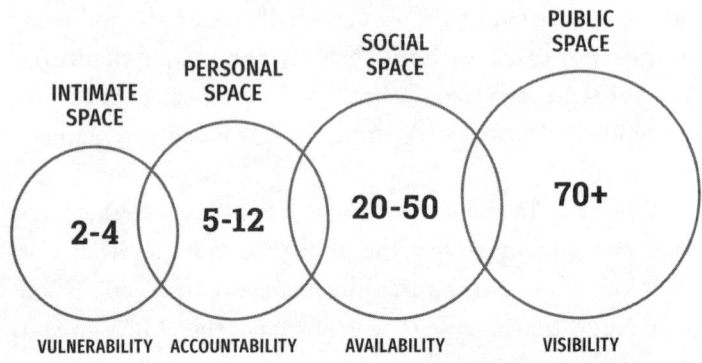

Source: JR Woodward and Dan White, *The Church as Movement: Starting and Sustaining Missional-Incarnational Communities* (Downers Grove, IL: InterVarsity Press, 2016), 156.

Intimate space is marked by raw vulnerability, the ability to have so much trust in another person that you can be your truest self and know they will treat you with care and compassion. In fresh expressions, intimate space can occur in the friendships that form among members of your group. This kind of interaction occurs in informal get-togethers between two to four people, like friends getting coffee and talking about their lives. We see Jesus exemplify this in his relationship with Peter, James, and John.

Personal space is a group of people who know each other well enough to hold each other accountable. In fresh expressions, this is the best space for discipleship to occur. In a group of five to twelve, everyone has the opportunity to speak their minds and be heard. Groups of this size will struggle to be outwardly focused and therefore have trouble bringing new people in, thus emphasizing the need for social space in a fresh expression network. Jesus exemplifies this space in his relationship with the twelve disciples.

Social space is geared toward authentic community and the accessibility of interactions with others. In fresh expressions, this will be important in the first two steps of the journey—it is the perfect space for building community early on. A group of twenty to fifty is easy to enter into as a new person and lends itself to fostering meaningful connections with individuals, which you will remember is what brings people back again. Social space is also where church takes shape. Worship occurs more naturally in this space where there is not an expectation of every voice being heard. In addition, this is the ideal size of a group participating in mission together. The early church concept of *oikos*, or extended families and friends gathered as house churches, exemplifies this space for us.

Public space is about sharing a common experience with a large group and being seen by others. These gatherings tend to be seventy or more people and therefore are too large to expect meaningful one-on-one interaction. It is usually a small number of people speaking or performing to a crowd. Most fresh expressions will not reach this space (except perhaps for the occasional one-time event). Remember, the average size of a fresh expression in the UK is forty-three.[142] Some however will reach this size and will need to remember this size of a gathering cannot function like the other spaces and succeed. Jesus exemplifies this space with his addresses to the crowds, like in the Sermon on the Mount.

A network of fresh expressions will incorporate multiple gatherings that include several of these spaces. Convergence, an artistic fresh expression of church connected to the Baptist General Association of Virginia, is a good example. In a given

---

142. Müller, "Fresh Expressions of Church and the Mixed Economy."

month they host art exhibits, art classes, and a performing arts group, offer art studio space, and rent out a recording studio for their neighbors in Alexandria, Virginia. In addition, they host a creative Bible study gathering, a Taizé worship service, and a monthly celebration where they eat together and share Communion.[143] During this season of virtual worship (brought about by the COVID-19 pandemic), they have developed artistic videos as a call to worship and fellowship online.[144]

By having multiple gatherings, we can create opportunities for folks to self-select based on their perceived needs at the time. For example, a seeker might come to the social gathering faithfully and the discipleship gathering on occasion, but as their faith grows, they might become more committed to the gatherings focused on the latter.

---

143. "Church," *Convergence*, accessed October 1, 2020, ourconvergence.org/faith/church.
144. "Learning to See Video Series," *VergeNow*, accessed October 1, 2020, verge-now.org/resources/learning-to-see-video-series/.

Chapter Seven | Doing It Again

Calvary Baptist of Bowling Green, VA

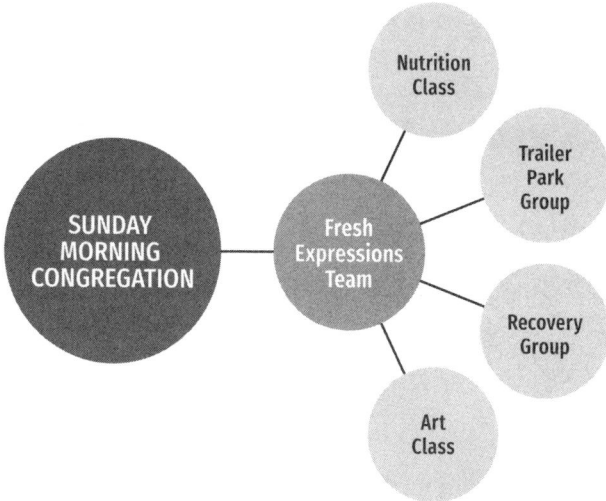

*Lines represent various forms of multidirectional tether

King Street Church and Boone UMC

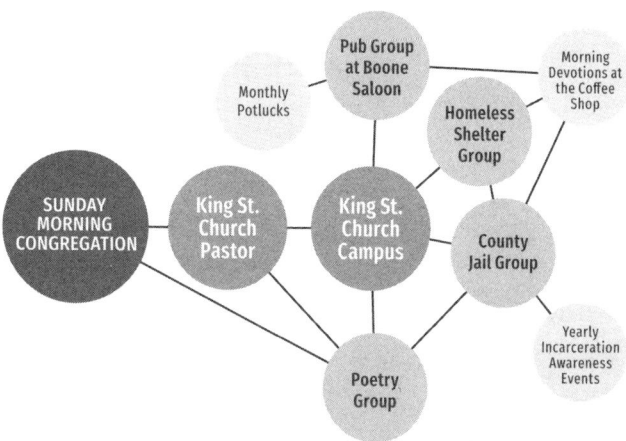

*Lines represent various forms of multidirectional tether

The Acts Network of First UMC Williamsport, PA

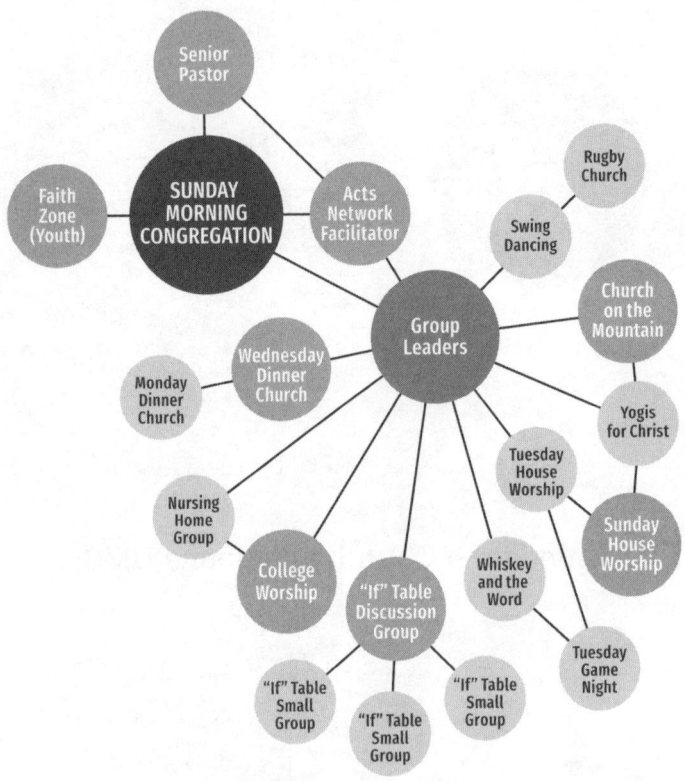

*Lines represent various forms of multidirectional tether

Movement Building on the Local Level

Identifying Potential Leaders. As your fresh expression is taking shape, you should look within your group for potential leaders who can start new fresh expressions. Who is bringing all of their friends? Who is taking initiative above and beyond what is expected of them? Who is a natural leader? Another source of potential leaders is your anchor church. One pastor I know frequently hosts a book study on fresh expressions topics at her anchor church. This helps her identify potential leaders and helps folks in her anchor church understand fresh expressions better. Here are a few things to look for in potential leaders:

- *Someone who hangs out on the periphery of your church.* The best leaders of fresh expressions are often unsettled in traditional forms of church. They might come late to worship and leave early. They might have gifts that have never been utilized and therefore they haven't been very involved in church leadership.
- *Someone with lots of friends outside the church.* Look for someone who is active in the surrounding community and has friends who don't go to church. They are a step ahead of folks who have become so ingrained in the congregation that they no longer know anyone outside the church.
- *Someone who speaks Christianese as a second language (or not at all).* When you become ingrained in church culture you can lose the ability to talk about your faith without using insider language. An essential skill in starting a fresh expression is the ability to have conversations about faith with people all over the spiritual and religious spectrum.
- *Someone who listens well.* Listening is essential throughout the fresh expressions journey. Therefore, don't look for the most eloquent orators in your church; look for the best listeners.

- *Someone who gathers people effortlessly.* Who throws the best parties at your church? They're likely able to bring a group together that could become a fresh expression.
- *Someone with spiritual velocity.* You know someone has this when the trajectory of their life is moving closer and closer to Jesus.[145] In other words, you don't have to be a Christian for ten years (or even two) to lead a fresh expression. Many fresh expressions are led by very young Christians because they are moving so fast toward Christ that they can't help but pull their friends along with them.[146]

There are also a few red flags to avoid in a potential leader. Watch out for someone on the outs with Christianity who is looking for an audience. And be wary of leaders with an unhealthy fixation on obedience and submission, as these can be signs of spiritual abuse.[147] Speaking of which, it's important that the members of a fresh expression know whom they can talk to at the anchor church if their leaders go astray.

Training New Leaders. Resourcing is all about providing someone with everything they need to succeed. You've started a fresh expression before, so you have an idea of what they will need. They might need some training in best practices. (If only there was a book about starting fresh expressions you could give them . . .) In addition, I have found the apprenticeship model to be helpful in training leaders from within your fresh expression. I've found the following concrete steps

---

145. Jon Ferguson, "3 Qualities of An Aspiring Apprentice," *Jon Ferguson*, accessed May 22, 2020, jonferguson.org/3-qualities-of-an-aspiring-apprentice/.
146. For more on leadership qualifications to look for, see Michael Moynagh, *Being Church, Doing Life* (Oxford, England: Monarch Books, 2014), 267.
147. Lisa Oakley and Kathryn Kinmond, *Breaking the Silence on Spiritual Abuse* (London: Palgrave Macmillan, 2013), 9–10.

Chapter Seven | Doing It Again

helpful for keeping me on track as I train someone to start a fresh expression.

1. I do, you watch, we talk.
2. I do, you help, we talk.
3. You do, I help, we talk.
4. You do, I watch, we talk.
5. You do, someone else watches.[148]

In the first step, you invite the new leader to observe how you lead. In each step, you take time to meet with the new leader one-on-one to talk and process how it went and see what questions they might have. The talk is the most important part of the whole process. In the second step, you invite the new leader to take a small part of leading the gathering. In the third step, you invite the new leader to take primary responsibility for the gathering, and you help. In the fourth step, the new leader hosts the whole gathering, and you become an observer. Don't forget to meet and process during each step! Lastly, the new leader begins to look for another leader they can apprentice, making this a multiplying movement.[149]

You can also offer training to a group of potential leaders. This is a good option for starting a network of fresh expressions at your anchor church. You can even break this book into an eight-week training for the group. The most important part of this process will be knowing what to hold onto tightly and what to hold loosely. It's important to have a vision for what your network of fresh expressions is about. If in the

---

148. Eric Metcalf, Nick Plassman, and Carter Moss, *Apprentice Field Guide*, (Naperville, IL: Community Christian Church, 2014), 43.
149. I am indebted to Brian Zehr of Intentional Impact for teaching me this simple and transformational process.

process of training a leader, you realize their vision doesn't fit well, you might need to tell them that it's a great idea, but it doesn't fit with what the network is trying to be, and they are welcome to pursue their vision on their own or connect with another ministry of the church. (See the denominational training section for some more ideas.)

Supporting Existing Leaders. As you shift from leading a fresh expression to leading a network, whether you have one leader or a dozen, you will need to make time to support your leaders. This can be a formal monthly meeting or a less formal dinner. It's good to have some brief training content, but the real focus of these meetings is to create space for people to voice frustrations, learn from failure, celebrate successes, and compare notes. Inviting folks to share best practices will help all of the other leaders. It will also be important to schedule regular one-on-one check-ins with your leaders.

As you can see, moving from a single fresh expression to a network is a lot of work. This is why I suggest that you only lead one fresh expression while leading a network. I learned this the hard way. As the pastor of King Street Church, I was active in co-leading up to five fresh expressions at a time. It began to take its toll as each fresh expression presented unique leadership challenges that required unique attention. I ended up having weeks where I was stretched far too thin. I've learned from folks like Mitch Marcello, lay staff person at First UMC in Williamsport, Pennsylvania, that if you lead only one or two fresh expressions, then you are able to support more leaders and multiply in greater numbers. Mitch's network is up to thirteen fresh expressions now!

Building Denominational Movements

In April 2019, Notre Dame in Paris caught fire. As some firefighters rushed to stop the blaze, others formed a human chain to rescue priceless religious relics from the burning church.[150] It might be extreme to say that our denominations are on fire, but they are certainly in trouble. A primary task of denominational leaders today reflects the work of these firefighters, finding the wisdom of our traditions collected over centuries, our great inheritance, and being willing to risk our own existence to pass them on to future generations. There's a remarkable statement in the "Book of Order of the Presbyterian Church (USA)" that reads, "The Church is to be a community of faith, entrusting itself to God alone, even at the risk of losing its life."[151]

I am a United Methodist minister; I carry with me the inherited wisdom of great Methodist theologians and evangelists such as John Wesley, Francis Asbury, Phoebe Palmer, Richard Allen, and Julia Foote, who carried the wisdom of those who came before them. Their understanding of grace has shaped the way I interact with God, the church, and the world. I've been formed in this particular tradition, a tradition that I long for others to experience and be formed by. I also realize that for this good old wine to be passed along in a post-Christian world, the wineskins need to change. Michael Moynagh calls this process "embodying the tradition."[152] What aspects of your tradition will you rush into the burning building for? Which ones are you willing to let go of? How will you pass along the ones you wish to keep in a rapidly changing world?

---

150. Jon Henley and Naaman Zhou, "Priest Helped Rescue Treasures from Burning Notre Dame," *The Guardian*, April 16, 2019, theguardian.com/world/2019/apr/16/notre-dame-fire-fears-over-fate-of-cathedrals-treasures.
151. Presbyterian Church (USA), "Book of Order 2019-2021," 2019, oga.pcusa.org/site_media/media/uploads/oga/pdf/2019-boo-elec_071219.pdf.
152. Michael Moynagh, *Being Church, Doing Life* (Oxford, England: Monarch Books, 2014), 283.

In our super-sized church minds, it might seem silly to invest so much into a movement that produces such small communities. And yet, as Dave Male, Director of Evangelism and Discipleship for the Church of England, writes, "This isn't about a few large communities but hundreds of small communities that are connecting effectively with people outside the Church."[153] For the cost of two traditional church plants, the Western North Carolina Conference has started 250 fresh expressions that have connected with some 5,000 people over the past three years. While only a small fraction of these folks would identify as Methodist, they have all been formed by the particulars of our tradition.

Identifying Potential Leaders. In building a regional Fresh Expressions movement, whether it is a whole state or a smaller region (like a county or city), the first step is to identify potential leaders and potential anchor churches. I have found several ways to do this:

1. Share the Vision. The first place to start is to share the vision of fresh expressions. Utilize social media to share articles, videos, and stories about fresh expressions in other regions. Host informational events about the vision of fresh expressions. Fresh Expressions US offers events called Vision Days. At a Vision Day, presenters share about how society is changing and how fresh expressions can respond to these changes. Be sure to follow up with attendees to see who resonated with the vision of fresh expressions and who didn't, and why. Learn more at freshexpressionsus.org/what-we-do.

2. Celebrate Early Adopters. After our first round of Vision Days in western North Carolina, we had a handful of churches in our conference that were interested

---

153. Dave Male, *How to Pioneer* (Grand Rapids: Monarch, 2014), 47.

in starting fresh expressions. We spent a year providing them with training and resources and then started to tell others in the conference about the work they were doing and the lives they were impacting. The most important part of storytelling is for potential leaders to see themselves in the stories you tell. This means featuring stories about fresh expressions leaders from a wide range of ages, races and ethnicities, genders, and church sizes, as well as featuring both clergy-led and laity-led initiatives. As you celebrate fresh expressions as a regional body, more churches will be inspired to step forward with ideas.

3. Host Participatory Events. The North Central District of the Florida Conference of the UMC hosted a one-time district-wide listening event. Churches that chose to participate were given instructions on how to do a day-long listening project in their community, and then invited to reflect with others on what they discovered.[154] At our yearly leadership gathering at the Western North Carolina Conference, we hosted several mock fresh expressions in the evening where potential leaders could experience firsthand what a fresh expression is like. I prefer this to having potential leaders visit actual fresh expressions in your region. Frequent visitors can become a burden on fresh expressions that are already dealing with delicate social dynamics.

4. Promote Replicable Models. In the next chapter, we will discuss in greater detail some models of fresh expressions that are easier to copy and paste. Models like dinner church, Messy Church, and pub theology are

---

154. Michael Beck, *Deep and Wild: Remissioning Your Church from the Outside* (Franklin, TN: Seedbed, 2021).

easier to understand for those who are intimidated by all of the possibilities of starting a fresh expression from scratch. Hosting regular informational events either in person or online around these models will pique the interest of people where generalized fresh expressions events might not.

5. Micro-grants. Fresh expressions do not require much of a budget to succeed. In the second year of our movement in western North Carolina, we offered $500 micro-grants to churches starting fresh expressions. We required each applicant to submit a paragraph describing their idea, attain approval from the church council, and have a fifteen-minute phone call conversation with me, in which I made sure it was actually a fresh expression they intended to start. We hoped for thirty, but had sixty-six churches start a fresh expression that year. This process ended up being one of our best ways to identify new churches to start fresh expressions. We have since changed our micro-grants to $250. The micro-grant works because it gets people's attention, and it also gives people permission to experiment with the support of the denomination. Our entrepreneurial leaders can say to their anchor churches, "See, I'm not crazy! Our Bishop wants us to be doing this."

Training New Leaders. As mentioned above, training is about making sure the churches and leaders in our region have what they need to start fresh expressions. Training churches in your region to start fresh expressions will be a mix of book learning and apprenticeship. Book studies via Facebook Live and Zoom can be a great way to start training leaders across the region. Fresh Expressions US offers more in-depth training and coaching through learning communities. At the Western North Carolina Conference, I try to offer regular trainings around fresh expressions basics, like the fresh expressions journey or the blended ecology. Be sure to have a mixture of online and in-person trainings and utilize homegrown experts as much as possible.

The Florida Conference of the United Methodist Church is also utilizing Fresh Expressions Studios, a training that includes the following:

1. *Shared Focus*: Learning is based on the fresh expressions journey.
2. *Self-Paced Discovery*: Teams learn using units in the *Godsend* app.[155]
3. *In-Person Check-Ins*: Twice a year all teams come together to do their planning together and to discuss the following:
    a. What has happened so far?
    b. What could we do next?
    c. What will we do next? (Build a plan.)
4. *Facebook Group*: Teams post these plans on a closed Facebook group and encourage each other as they go.
5. *Coaching*: Teams receive Zoom-based coaching to help overcome bumps and challenges.[156]

Supporting Existing Leaders. Offering peer-support groups based around geography and affinity is an essential aspect of building a healthy Fresh Expressions movement. In western

---

155. "Growing New Christian Communities: Godsend," *Fresh Expressions* (December 2018), freshexpressions.org.uk/2018/12/27/growing-new-christian-communities-godsend/.
156. Michael Adam Beck, "Mike Moynagh: Florida Conference Studio Introduction," YouTube video, 14:22, July 16, 2020, youtube.com/watch?v=G5jTwQwk4Q0&app=desktop.

Becoming Church

North Carolina, our goal is for each district to have what we call a practitioner group, where leaders of Fresh Expressions have the opportunity to share best practices, celebrate success, and process failure. Florida Conference's district groups utilize a series of questions whenever they meet:

1. What are some of the things we celebrated over the past month or year?
2. What have some of our struggles been?
3. What are some of the things we would like to see happen over the next month or year?
4. What do we need to do to make these happen?[157]

In addition to district groups, we have begun gathering groups of leaders who are focused on similar affinities (e.g., dinner churches, pub churches, Messy Churches).

I have found the research around communities of practice to be helpful in shaping these gatherings. According to educational theorists Etienne and Beverly Wenger-Trayner, "Communities of practice are groups of people who share a concern or a passion for something they do and learn how to do it better as they interact regularly."[158] As leaders of fresh expressions come together regularly, they begin to share experiences, are inspired by new ideas, and find ways to address recurring problems.

These gatherings are the best part of my job. In the gatherings, fresh expression leaders can be themselves and receive

---

157. For more on the Florida Conference's Fresh Expressions Movement, see Michael Beck and Jorge Acevedo, *A Field Guide to Methodist Fresh Expressions* (Nashville: Abingdon, 2020).
158. Etienne and Beverly Wenger-Trayner, "Introduction to Communities of Practice," *Wenger-Trayner*, 2015, wenger-trayner.com/introduction-to-communities-of-practice/.

much-needed support from their peers. The meetings are filled with laughter and comments like, "Yes, you get it!" I've also noticed that leaders who have been in their fresh expressions longer are able to mentor folks who are newer to the process.

Conclusion

The denominational church in the United States is facing a great adaptive challenge. Ron Heifetz, founder of the Center for Public Leadership, reflects,

> An adaptive challenge requires people to distinguish between what is precious and essential and what is expendable within their culture. In cultural adaptation, the job is to take the best from history, leave behind that which is no longer serviceable, and through innovation learn ways to thrive in the new environment. Therefore, adaptive work is inherently conservative as well as progressive. The point of innovation is to conserve what is best from history as the community moves into the future.[159]

As we venture into our changing world, we as churches must choose what is essential and find creative ways to carry these things into our new reality. Starting a Fresh Expressions movement is one way to do this.

---

159. Ron A. Heifetz , "Adaptive Work," *Kansas Leadership Center Journal*, (Spring 2010), hesston.edu/wp-content/uploads/2017/12/KLCAdaptiveWork.pdf.

Further Reading:

JR Woodward and Dan White Jr., *Church as Movement: Starting and Sustaining Missional-Incarnational Communities* (Downers Grove, IL: InterVarsity Press, 2016).

Woodward and White have put together a textbook for Christian movement-making. It's the book you'll turn to when trying to figure out how to lead and organize a budding network of fresh expressions.

Jeremy Heimans and Henry Timms, *New Power: How Anyone Can Persuade, Mobilize, and Succeed in Our Chaotic, Connected Age* (New York: Anchor Books, 2018).

Few books have changed the way I lead as much as this one. Heimans and Timms witness to the changing power dynamics of the digital age. While *old power* was held by the few and tightly guarded, *new power* is distributed and participatory. This book can help you unleash participatory power in your church or denomination.

Accompanying Prayer
A Collect for Doing It Again

O Christ, you ended your ministry on earth by sending out apprentices to carry on your work in a host of new forms and settings. Remind us of how the things we take most for granted were once fresh expressions of church. Give us the joy of Paul as we witness and pray with grandparents' affection for all of the communities that start downstream of our own work. We thank you for the honor of being made recipients, leaders, and bestowers of the earthly work of our Creator, who reigns with you and the Holy Spirit, one God, who was and is and is to come. *Amen.*

— Terry Stokes

Chapter Eight

FLIP-FLOPS AND FINAL THOUGHTS

*"I may not have gone where I intended to go, but
I think I have ended up where I needed to be."*
— Douglas Adams

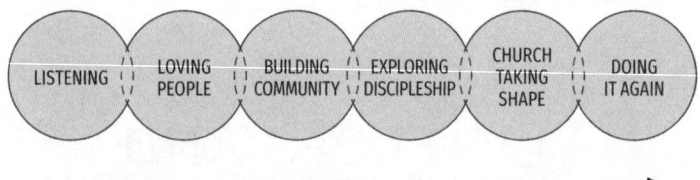

UNDERPINNED BY PRAYER AND CONTINUING CONNECTION TO THE WIDER CHURCH

With an exponential increase of thru-hikers on the Appalachian Trail every year, something called "flip-flop thru-hiking" has gained popularity. No, it's not about your footwear. A flip-flop thru-hiker starts at a point in the middle of the 2,000-mile trail, often Harpers Ferry, West Virginia. They hike to the northern terminus in Maine, fly back to Harpers Ferry, and hike down to the southern terminus in Georgia. This allows the hiker to avoid crowds and makes for much more pleasant weather than a traditional thru-hike. It might seem like a less romantic journey, not getting to end with the famous Mt. Katahdin picture. But one flip-flop hiker reflects, "No matter when you reach it, Katahdin is a tremendous accomplishment and you'll treasure your Katahdin pic and share it with everyone you know. Each state crossing was just as important to me even if it didn't occur in the same order as most hikers. And you can always create your own milestone pics as needed."[160] While a purist might turn up their nose at starting in the middle, she completed the journey with no regrets. Everyone knows purists are annoying anyway.

The fresh expressions journey looks pretty cut-and-dry on paper. I mean, it's six circles in a straight line. It's clear

---

160. Carla Robertson, "10 Reasons You'll Love a Flip Flop Thru Hike," *The Trek*, September 24, 2015, thetrek.co/10-reasons-youll-love-a-flip-flop-thru-hike/.

Chapter Eight | Flip-Flops and Final Thoughts

there's a "right" order. The problem is we're trekking with the Holy Spirit, and as Jesus says, "The wind blows wherever it pleases."[161] All that to say, your fresh expressions journey might move through the steps in a nice sequential manner, but there's a good chance it will be far more unpredictable. Here are a few ways it might look different.

Starting in the Middle

Sherrie is a retired deacon in the United Methodist Church, but like most recently retired clergy I know, she's far from finished serving. Her husband, Alan, is a naturalist, and a few years ago, they had the idea to start a church out in nature. They combined their gifts to create the Smoky Mountain Hiking Community in Waynesville, North Carolina, in the spring of 2019. Before their first hike, Sherrie reflected that they already had friends who were not affiliated with any church who were interested in hiking and talking about faith. They started hosting hikes twice a month, beginning with a devotional reflection at the trailhead. After a few months, they realized that they needed a way to invite new people in. They began to host one devotional hike a month and one social hike that served as a place to build community with folks who were not ready to talk about faith.

Everyone's fresh expressions journey is unique. Wherever you start, you'll be starting in a different place than everyone else. You might have a ton of connections in your community already, or you might not have any. Perhaps you have been listening without knowing it for years. Perhaps you built a community without thinking it could become a church. Jump in where you are and start walking forward. Like Sherrie and Alan, you might need to look backward in the

---

161. John 3:8.

fresh expressions journey for some ideas to fill out what your fresh expression is missing.

Fresh Initiatives

In third grade, my wife received a note from a boy that read, "Will you be my girlfriend? If no, tell Ali I love her." You should always be prepared for things not to go as planned. As I mentioned in previous chapters, to traverse the fresh expressions journey without manipulating the people you connect with, you always have to be open to the group ceasing to move toward church.[162] If the group of at-risk youth skaters doesn't want to explore discipleship, God is still making things new by creating a safe space for them to experience unconditional love. For the sake of clarity, however, we wouldn't call this a fresh expression. We would call it a fresh initiative. It's a community where people can experience belonging, but it's not moving toward becoming a church.

Bridgebacks

One of the first lessons drilled into my head about fresh expressions was that a fresh expression is not meant to be a steppingstone for people to come to your Sunday morning service. However, while it's important to create a fresh expression with the intention of forming a new church for the people you are connecting with, you might end up being a bridge to traditional church for some people. There's no sense in fighting it when that happens. Senior pastor and fresh expression leader Michael Beck has embraced "bridgebacks" by creating a Sunday morning service that mixes the best of traditional

---

162. Michael Moynagh, *Being Church, Doing Life* (Oxford, England: Monarch Books, 2014), 135.

church and fresh expressions in a service called New Life.[163] At King Street Church, we had folks who were disconnected from church for years spend time with us for a year, and then start attending a different church where their friends worshiped. It might not have been good for our attendance rolls at Boone UMC, but it was a kingdom win. It's not the way fresh expressions are designed to work, but remember, purists are annoying.

Replicable Models

Some people like a blank canvas; others like adult coloring books. In the fresh expressions world, the blank canvas is creating a fresh expression from scratch, one that is completely unique to the context in which you live. The adult coloring books are replicable models that are easier to cut and paste in a wide variety of contexts. Here are a few:

Dinner Church. Dinner church is simply the church gathered around the dinner table. Some dinner churches are large gatherings in church fellowship halls or large community spaces; some are smaller gatherings meeting in restaurants or homes. Orders of worship vary from dinner church to dinner church. Some include short messages, some encourage table conversations, some offer Communion, most have a time of community prayer, some have music, and some don't. All have an intentional focus on inviting neighbors who are not connected to a church. If your church already has a feeding ministry, it's not a big jump to become a dinner church! This is the lowest hanging fruit I've seen for a fresh expression. What church doesn't already feed people?

---

163. Michael Adam Beck, *Deep Roots, Wild Branches* (Franklin, Tennessee: Seedbed Publishing, 2019), 139.

Messy Church. You would be hard-pressed to find a church that doesn't desire more families with children in their congregation. Messy Church has proven to be one of the most effective ways to bring in families of all shapes, sizes, and ages in a post-Christian world. According to their website,

> Messy Church is a form of church for children and adults that involves creativity, celebration and hospitality.... It typically includes a welcome; a long creative time to explore the biblical theme through [crafts and activities]; a short celebration time involving story, prayer, song, games; and a sit-down meal together at tables.[164]

They are by far the most prominent and fruitful model of fresh expressions, representing nearly a third of all fresh expressions in the UK.[165] There's even a version for adapting it to nursing homes called Messy Vintage.

Lucy Moore, the founder of Messy Church in the UK, shared this story:

> A Messy Church leader told me recently of a family who had started coming to their Messy Café outreach project because their five-year-old was asking about God; the family then came to Messy Church, joined the Sunday congregation too, are on the Messy leadership team and are now asking to be baptized. They've brought six extended family members into the church by enthusiastic invitation and they want to help raise

---

164. "What Messy Church Is and Isn't," *Messy Church*, accessed June 4, 2020, messychurch.org.uk/what-messy-church-and-isnt.
165. George Lings, "The Day of Small Things," *Church Army* (November 2016), churcharmy.org/Publisher/File.aspx?ID=204265.

money for Messy Church. If this isn't discipleship, what is?[166]

Most Messy Churches meet once a month in a community space outside the church, but some meet in church fellowship halls. Some dinner churches in western North Carolina that meet weekly are incorporating a Messy Church once a month.

Messy Church is a ton of fun. Johannah Myers, Director of Christian Formation at Aldersgate UMC in Greenville, South Carolina, tells the story of a group of seventy-year-old men from the church who were arguing over who got to lead the "fun activity" at the next Messy Church. One of the men, who doesn't have grandchildren of his own, told her, "If it wasn't for Messy Church, I wouldn't get to interact with kids, and that is so special."[167] Not only is their Messy Church the most intergenerational worship gathering at the church, those in attendance also reflect the rich diversity of the surrounding community.

While Messy Church is a blast, fair warning: it requires a significant amount of preparation, and if you meet in the fellowship hall, the combination of glue, glitter, and children won't make you any friends among the church trustees. For more information, check out messychurchusa.org.

Memory Café. Trinity United Methodist Church in Gastonia, North Carolina, wanted to be more active in their community, and as they got to know their community, they learned about the challenges facing their neighbors with memory issues. Alzheimer's and dementia can be incredibly

---

166. "Playfully Serious," *Church Army* (January 2019), churcharmy.org/Publisher/File.aspx?ID=225713.
167. Johannah Myers (Director of Christian Formation, Aldersgate UMC) in discussion with the author, January 2021.

isolating for those experiencing it and their caretakers. The church reached out to local agencies who were active in this area, and it was suggested that their church host a Memory Café. One social worker defines it this way,

> Memory Cafés are welcoming social gatherings for people with dementia and their care partners. They meet in safe and accessible community spaces and include activities aimed at a wide range of cognitive abilities. They often include sing-alongs, gentle exercise, art, socializing, drumming, storytelling, and dancing.[168]

Memory Café is not a religious gathering, but it can be a great way to connect with folks in your community with dementia and their care partners. Out of these connections, some churches are inviting folks back for a worship service that is designed especially for them.

Pub Theology. There's something about church in a bar that piques the curiosity of those outside the church. "Your church meets in a bar? That doesn't sound like the churches I know." As I mentioned earlier, a little distance from preconceived notions of church is a good thing for most people outside the church. The pub is a place where long conversations about life happen naturally, so it's a perfect location for discipleship to occur. PubTheology.com makes starting a group easy with a starter kit and weekly discussion topics.[169]

---

168. Beth Soltzberg, "Starting Your Memory Café," *Act on Alzheimer's*, accessed May 30, 2017, actonalz.org/sites/default/files/documents/Starting%20Your%20Memory%20Cafe%20-%20A%20tour%20through%20the%20toolkit%2C%205-30-17.pdf.
169. "Resources," *Pub Theology*, accessed June 22, 2020, pubtheology.com/resources/.

I am often asked about mixing alcohol and church. As a leader you will need to be careful to exemplify responsibility with alcohol, and you will need to talk to attendees right away if they begin straying from such responsibility. In my six years at King Street Church, it only happened a few times. Each time I took the person aside and said, "Hey, I noticed you drank more than everyone else around the table. Is everything okay?" Both times it led to a disclosure of some serious stuff happening in their lives and the individual apologizing for breaking the norms of the group. Addiction is not something to take lightly. If you are worried about someone in your group, seek the advice of someone who is in your local recovery community. You can find leaders of local chapters of Alcoholics Anonymous at aa.org.

Recovery Groups/Services. We are all in recovery from something. The apostle Paul says in his letter to the Romans, "For all have sinned and fall short of the glory of God."[170] Nearly one in ten Americans struggles with drug or alcohol addiction.[171] Many churches across the country have created faith communities around recovery. Celebrate Recovery is the most prolific version of this and provides resources for starting and sustaining groups. Be sure to connect with and partner with existing recovery programs in your community before you start something new. Even if you are not starting a recovery group, it's good for every leader to familiarize yourself with the language of recovery. The recovery movement

---

170. Romans 3:23.
171. "New Data Show Millions of Americans with Alcohol and Drug Addiction Could Benefit from Health Care Reform," *Partnership to End Addiction*, accessed March 29, 2020, drugfree.org/learn/drug-and-alcohol-news/new-data-show-millions-of-americans-with-alcohol-and-drug-addiction-could-benefit-from-health-care-reform/.

created by Alcoholics Anonymous is a remarkable contribution to the church and our understanding of God's grace.

Giving Circles. A giving circle is a group of people who gather together to pool financial resources and give those resources to an agreed-upon social cause. Some are groups of friends or coworkers, others gather strangers around a shared concern about a particular social issue, and others gather neighbors together.[172] By pooling resources, people feel like their giving makes a bigger difference, and it's a great way to build community as well. There are many ways to do collecting and granting, but one easy way is to utilize mygrowfund.org/giving-circles. Collective giving is going to sound familiar to church folks—a giving circle is basically a fun and hip version of a missions committee. As the group gathers, look for opportunities to talk about the spiritual elements of generosity. Jesus has plenty to say about giving that you can bring to the group for reflection.

These models of fresh expressions are easier to "cut and paste," but it's still important to think through your local context. It's vital to ask if this model is the right fit for your community and your church. Then talk through how this fresh expression will need to look different to fit well in your context. One dinner church in our conference connects with folks experiencing homelessness, one is connecting with the elderly, and another is connecting with truck driving school students. As you can imagine they all look a little different. For any fresh expression to succeed, you'll need to build relationships with your neighbors first and build partnerships with other

---

172. "Guide to Giving Circles: Pooling Resources to Support Change and Build Community with Joelle Berman and LiJia Gong," *Get Together*, audio, podcasts.apple.com/us/podcast/guide-to-giving-circles-pooling-resources-to-support/id1447445682?i=1000477241485.

organizations that are connecting with people in your community. Focusing on the program over the relationships is a sure-fire way to create another gathering full of church people.

Fresh Measurements of Success

Measurement creates meaning. I've heard it said that if you don't measure what matters, what you measure will become what matters. While wild and rebellious fresh expression leaders will resist anything that feels institutional, measurements will help your anchor church understand your vision and celebrate your successes. And—trust me—you want to define success at the beginning, otherwise your anchor church will use old measurements, and it won't be pretty.[173]

Help your anchor church understand that a fresh expression is not about getting more people there on Sunday. It's about connecting your church with people who would never even think about coming on Sunday morning. Share stories of transformation that you witness in your fresh expression with your anchor church (in a way that maintains confidentiality). Feed them to your senior pastor so she can include them as sermon illustrations. This will help your anchor church to understand that it's not about big numbers; it's about the lost sheep being found. The Good Shepherd still leaves the ninety-nine for just one sheep! If your fresh expression connects with six people who were not connected with the church, that's a big deal—better than 600 church people who never left, according to kingdom math!

Measurements can also help you see if you're moving toward your vision. I heard of one church that counted cigarette butts in the parking lot after their recovery service as

---

173. For an in-depth look at evaluation in fresh expressions, see Moynagh, *Being Church, Doing Life* (Oxford, England: Monarch Books, 2014), 326–344.

a measurement. More cigarettes meant they were connecting with more of the people to whom God had called them. Forget counting butts in pews—count butts in the parking lot.

Dinner churches and Messy Churches might have a check-in table, but for most fresh expressions I would not suggest passing an attendance pad. Instead, as the leader, jot down who is in attendance, and when you get home, add it to a spreadsheet. At King Street Church, I did a monthly review of who was present and who had dropped off. It gave me an opportunity to reach out to those we hadn't seen in a while.

Life Cycles

At some point every thru-hike on the Appalachian Trail ends. Whether it's at Mt. Katahdin or elsewhere, pilgrims stand next to a sign for a photo with hands raised and say, "My job is done." While the church universal will never end, most local churches will. Fresh expressions are even more likely to move through a complete lifecycle, declaring at some point that their work in the kingdom is done.

How do you know a fresh expression is coming to an end? The clearest way to tell is if it ceases to bring in new people. This is true of any church, but larger churches take a lot longer to end this way. Lovett Weems speaks of churches that move forward like a car that ran out of gas. If they are moving fast, they can roll for a long time, but it's still just coasting. When you have a fresh expression of twenty people and you cease to bring new people in, don't expect the coasting to last long. Another way a fresh expression ends is when the leader loses steam. At King Street Church we had an incredible fresh expression forming with single moms. When the leader needed to focus on work and family, we didn't have another leader ready, and the group fizzled. We celebrated what God had done through her, and we knew her ministry would carry on in new ways.

Some fresh expressions will live a brief life cycle, lasting less than a year. However, in a network of fresh expressions these dying groups can give birth to new ones. At King Street Church, we often sent out leaders to start new groups. Some lasted; others did not. If their groups didn't take off, we welcomed the leaders back, celebrated their experiment, figured out what we could learn, and tried again. Established churches can rarely afford to fail, but fresh expressions can take risks, fail faster, and grow our wisdom.

Conclusion

There's a beautiful simplicity to the Appalachian Trail. You walk a well-worn path, albeit a difficult one, following the little white blazes for 2,000 miles. It's this simplicity that drew me to the fresh expressions journey. We listen to our neighborhood, increasing our understanding of the lives of our neighbors. We form friendships with the people we meet and deepen our existing ones. The friendships that grow deeper give way to a new community—a group of people bound together by a common purpose. In this newly formed community, the Holy Spirit opens hearts and minds to a new way of understanding, and people's eyes are opened to the presence of Christ that has always been among them. We show our friends what it looks like to live like Jesus, and over time we become a church. As we walk this journey together, the Spirit inspires members of the group to begin their own communities. It's not complicated, and it doesn't require an advanced theological degree. Nor is it easy. Community is messy, and there are situations that require great resilience and courage. And yet, we do not journey alone.

The prophets Isaiah and Micah proclaim a beautiful song for our journey:

> Come, let us go up to the mountain of the Lord,
> to the temple of the God of Jacob.
> He will teach us his ways,
> so that we may walk in his paths.[174]

As you journey forward, may you walk in the path of Christ, who shows us what it looks like to build a community that moves throughout the world, proclaiming the Good News to all those we encounter along the way. You may not save your church. That was never the goal anyway. You may do something even more important. You may discover a new way of being the church. You may even discover a new way of being human.

Happy trails!

---

174. Isaiah 2:3; see also Micah 4:2.

Further Reading:

Michael Moynagh, *Being Church, Doing Life: Creating Gospel Communities Where Life Happens* (Oxford, England: Monarch Books, 2014).

If you are looking for a deeper dive into the fresh expressions journey, this book is a perfect next step. Moynagh is a prominent theologian in the Fresh Expressions movement in the UK, and this book is full of helpful concepts and examples to add to your fresh expressions toolbox. For an updated version of his work, you can check out the *Godsend* app available in your mobile phone app store.

Jason Jennings, *The High-Speed Company: Creating Urgency and Growth in a Nanosecond Culture* (New York: Portfolio, 2015).

Whether you're leading a fresh expression, a network of fresh expressions, a church, or a denominational organization, you need to clearly define your purpose, set your values, and measure your success. Jennings provides a helpful guide to doing this well.

Accompanying Prayer
A Collect for the End of a Journey

O God, you rested from your completed work of creation and remarked that it was very good. And yet some of the things you created lived short lives. For however long the life of our communities turn out to be, at their end show us how to rest and reflect on the goodness that you created. For those that produce seed that brings forth other new life, we praise you.

For those whose death teaches us new and better ways to cultivate, we praise you. And whenever we arrive at the end of our journey, we will raise an ebenezer to mark what you have done and how far we have come by the guiding grace of the Holy Spirit, who reigns with you our Father and our Lord Jesus Christ, one God, now and forever. *Amen.*

— Terry Stokes

ABOUT THE AUTHOR

LUKE EDWARDS is the Associate Director of Church Development for the Western North Carolina Conference of the United Methodist Church and a trainer for Fresh Expressions US. He is an Elder in Full Connection in the United Methodist Church. He was the founding pastor of King Street Church, a network of fresh expressions in Boone, North Carolina. He grew up in an area of western Massachusetts that was recently named the most post-Christian metropolitan area in the United States, where he joined his first micro-faith community at the age of fourteen. Between his upbringing and his work in local, regional, and national levels of the Fresh Expressions movement, Luke has a unique perspective into how creating micro-communities can offer a path for the future of the church in a post-Christian society. He lives in Huntersville, North Carolina, where he enjoys going for walks in the woods with his wife and daughter. His blog and podcast can be found at www.faithfulcommunity.com.